About the Author

In 2004 **Nikki McArthur** (with her husband and three children), traded in her life as an IT trainer and hotelier in the UK, to live the good life in rural Southwest France. She now has five children, is a freelance proof reader, runs a retreat and holiday rentals, garden centre/ landscaping business, and has also found the time to pursue her love for writing.

This is the first in the "A mother in France" series, the second of which is entitled "No time Toulouse! A family living in France" and is due to be released in 2021.

She has also contributed to the anthology "I've got something to say", produced by the writing group Women's Voices Southwest France.

Nikki writes a blog at www.amotherinfrance.com and you can also follow her @AmotherinFrance on Facebook, Instagram and Twitter

What have we got Toulouse?

A family moving to France

Nikki McArthur

Published in 2020 by AmotherinFrance.com Publishing
Escanecrabe, France

ISBN: 978-2-9568087-0-1

Cover and illustrations by KikiWoodDesign.com

Acknowledgements

I would like to thank everyone who has helped me through the process of writing this book, with special thanks to Michelle Martinez for her encouragement and tips.

Thanks to Kiki Wood for her wonderful illustrations, cover design and logo.

Finally, much love and thanks to my family for giving me endless material to write about and without whom this book would never have been written in the first place.

Contents

Foreword

When we were in the process of moving to France with a young family, I longed to read about others' experiences to find out what life would really be like. None of the many books I read satisfied this urge. They were all written largely by retirees and whilst they gave an insight into living in France, I knew that my life would be very different from the experiences I was reading about. I wanted to know what it was like to have a baby, what the schools were like, how my children might adapt, what problems we may face as a family and how we might make a living. None of these needs were ever satisfied and so I vowed to myself I would write the book I would have found most useful. Once I started writing I found I had so many experiences to share that it became too big for one book and so I have split it into a series of books. In this first book – What have we got Toulouse – A family moving to France, I share the reasons for moving, how we found and bought our house and what we discovered in the early years.

So here it is. Our experiences of why we moved to France, how we did it and what happened when we got there. I hope you find it interesting, inspiring, entertaining and most of all useful.

PART 1

Moving to France

What have we got Toulouse?

A family in England

September 2004

"We're finally going Nicks"

"I know, I can't quite believe it's happening. We're going to France... we're actually going to **live** in France!" I replied. It hardly seemed possible.

We had just lived through six months of stress and uncertainty; our dream of living abroad seemed to be turning into a nightmare. Finally, however, Gary felt he could allow himself to get excited. Being the more cautious, 'sensible shoe' half of our marriage, I couldn't help feeling more than a little anxious at the thought of all we had ahead of us.

We were standing in the conservatory of our guest house on the Kent coast, looking out over our tiny garden. We had cooked and cleared up breakfasts for twenty and the last of our guests had just shuffled their way out of the dining room.

"Phew, I thought they'd never go!" I sighed. It had been fun running a guest house, but the monotony of it was exhausting; having to cook and serve full English breakfasts every morning, cleaning rooms, shopping and cooking evening meals, waiting for guests to arrive and manning the bar in the evening. In addition, we both had other part-time jobs (Gary was a freelance lecturer in Horticulture, and I was an IT trainer) not to mention three young children, so life was hectic and a constant juggle between guests, work and family. Our days seemed never ending and we had hardly any time for ourselves or the children. Then there were the guests, some of whom were challenging to say the least... One guest had once spent half an hour telling us every detail of the local bus timetable. It's not easy trying to look fascinated whilst suppressing the urge to scream "Here's an idea, before you start telling a story make sure it HAS A POINT!" We had some interesting guests. There was the poor old man who had an aroma of "eau de toilette" in a literal sense. Unfortunately, his trousers fell down one morning in the breakfast room (the string snapped). Then there was the couple whose dog had puppies on the brand-new sofa bed in room number 2 – it was OK though as she mopped up the mess with the new white bath towels!

Back in the conservatory, outside was overcast and chilly. It didn't seem possible that only a few weeks earlier we'd been sitting on the sea wall eating fish and chips and watching the boys splash about in the sea. Yes, there were advantages to living in a seaside town and we did manage to escape the monotony sometimes (albeit briefly). I remember the seagulls circling overhead waiting for our leftovers. Strange how when we'd first moved to the coast three years earlier their raucous cries had often disturbed me in the early hours. After a while it just became background noise and I hardly noticed them anymore. I wondered what sounds we might experience in our new home in the French countryside. I imagined being woken by the distant crow of a cockerel and the sound of running water. Little did I know that I was more likely to be rudely awoken by a cacophony of frogs and the howling of the dogs of the local hunt!

I glanced across at Gary, now lost in his own thoughts. Finally, one of his ultimate goals was coming to fruition. A passionate and knowledgeable horticulturist who loved nature and his family, and at forty-two was the hardest working person I had ever known. If anyone deserved a break in life, he did. His physical and mental strength had been put to the test many times, and yet his enormous sense of adventure and belief that we could achieve anything we set out to do, was the main reason we'd managed to get to this point. Many others would have given up long before.

We'd been through a lot in our lives and had had several new beginnings, but this was a bigger step than we had ever taken before; something many people only fantasise about, something I had thought for many years was only a pipe dream for us. But, despite everything, we achieved the seemingly impossible, and now it really was happening. We were about to trade in our current life for a completely new one in another country. We were packing up belongings, kids and dogs and moving over 1,000 km south to a country we'd only ever visited before, where we knew no one and hardly spoke the language. Were we completely mad? I'm sure many people thought we were, but no, not mad, just restless and disillusioned with the life we had and desperate to find a better one for our growing family. As I stood there pondering what life had in store for us this time, I reflected on the past few years and how we had arrived at this point...

Where it all began

O ur first thoughts of living abroad date back to 1985 when three months after we first met, we took our first holiday together. Gary was twenty-two, working as an Assistant Manager of a garden centre and living in a rented house with a fellow colleague in Kent. I was just eighteen and working as a Secretary in London and living at home with my parents, just a few miles down the road from him. As Gary worked every weekend, it was down to me to book our holiday.

In those days there was no Internet and the most popular and easiest way to book a holiday was a package deal through a travel agent. I sat in the travel agents in Faversham High Street while the assistant trawled through the deals on the computer. It was July and we had both booked two weeks off work the following week and were happy to go anywhere "I don't care where we go, as long as it's hot and cheap" were Gary's only instructions.

After turning down a couple of offers to Ibiza and Majorca, the travel agent came up with a last-minute deal to the Greek island of Crete the following Saturday. I'd never visited Greece but had seen the deep blue skies, crisp sandy beaches and charming white square buildings in the glossy travel brochures on my parents' coffee table. So, before I knew it, I'd said "Yes", handed over the cheque and the holiday was booked.

I was so excited; I rushed outside to the phone box and rang Gary at work.

"I've booked it. We're going to Crete on Saturday. Only £99 for two weeks", I blurted out.

"Oh wow, that's amazing, can't wait" was Gary's enthusiastic response.

The two-week holiday was unforgettable. Well, actually the accommodation was awful. A very basic room, two hard single beds, shared communal showers and toilets that Gary had to unblock every morning before I would use them, but we really didn't care. We fell in love with the island and the Greeks, the heat, the pace of life, the azure skies and the crystal-clear seas. "This is the life", we thought, and this was the life we wanted. The warm evenings, strolling around the harbour in Chania, eating outside, the food, the smell of rosemary, suntan oil and sunshine; the taste of olives, feta, tzatziki, moussaka, baklava, yoghurt and fresh honey; the sounds of the sea lapping against the shore, the church bells chiming and the clang of the roaming sheep and goats never far away. We loved it all.

One day we hired mopeds and we drove for the day to Knossos (ancient Minoan remains). Travelling along the breathtaking coastline is something I will never forget. Even two days bed ridden with sunstroke and the agonising pain of sunburn couldn't spoil the magic of that holiday and the impact it would have on our entire lives together. We had met on a blind date arranged by mutual friends just three months earlier and we both knew very early on that we had found our match.

The seed of living a life abroad had been sown, but at that particular time we had no savings and no way of making a living there, our only option was to make some money before we could pursue this other life.

We left our respective homes a year later and moved to Surrey where Gary had been offered a job to start up a small nursery from scratch for a lady who owned a florist shop. Our first home together was a flat above a stable. Not that you could really call it a flat, it was more of a barn. It had a chemical loo and no bathroom. We had to go over to Mrs B's house (the owner) to have a bath and do our washing. The sink in the tiny kitchen area wasn't plumbed into a drain. It had a bucket under it which I was forever forgetting to empty. I'd pull the plug from the sink after washing up and then suddenly realise the bucket under was already full and all the water would spill out onto the floor. The cooker was an old electric one with an eye level grill with only one setting working which was very hot. Most of my early experiments with cooking were burnt offerings scraped from pans –

not helped by the fact that the only pans we had were very thin and poor quality from the Catalogue Reject shop.

We soon discovered that the previous occupants of the flat were still in residence. The green velvet curtains that once hung on the only window in the space that was our bedroom come sitting room, lay in a heap on the floor. I picked them up and mouse droppings showered from the numerous holes in the lining. Undeterred, we set traps for the mice. We didn't get much sleep that first night, and not for the usual reasons a young couple would be up half the night. We were disturbed every ten minutes all night long by the sound of the traps snapping left, right and centre and Gary jumped up each time to reset them.

I suppose we should have known that this venture was doomed from the start. The night before we left, we had packed up Gary's precious Volkswagen Golf with all our worldly belongings. It didn't amount to much – a few clothes, a few hastily bought cooking utensils and a Delia Smith cookery course book which was a present from my sister (I still have and use it– it's my bible). When we awoke the next morning, Gary was feeling rough – temperature, aching all over, typical flu-like symptoms, so I had to drive the two-hour journey to Cranleigh in Surrey. The illness continued for several months and yet Gary carried on working through it. It was eventually discovered he had glandular fever. Every day he would work hard preparing the land for opening the nursery, employing staff, etc., and then collapse in bed with exhaustion at the end of the day. I don't know how he did it.

Soon after arriving, I got a job at a local removals company as a shorthand secretary. We made some friends, but our life in Surrey was far from smooth. One day when Gary was working in the nursery a smartly dressed guy came up to him.

"I'm from Surrey Highways, we are resurfacing down the road and may have some tarmac over. I notice there are a few holes in your driveway and wondered, if we have any surplus tarmac, would you like us to fill the holes?".

Gary explained that he was not the owner, but he gave Mrs B a call at her florist shop and explained. Mrs B was very interested but didn't want the whole drive done – just a few of the biggest potholes filled up. Gary relayed the information to the highways' guy and went off to carry on with his work. Later that day, he went to investigate the sound of a large vehicle nearby only to discover they had nearly covered half the entire driveway – not just the potholes he had indicated. Gary insisted they stop as that was not at all what he had asked for and he had a horrible feeling this was going to cost more than they had bargained for. The men grudgingly stopped and returned that evening with the bill. Well, it was of course a substantial amount which Mrs B was not prepared to pay, and we had obviously been conned. The men were not from Surrey Highways after all. After much posturing and threats, Mrs B struck a deal with some old silk flowers she had in storage and the men begrudgingly left.

A few days later we had been out for the evening and had parked the car in the car park outside the barn before going up to the flat. We were just settling down into bed when we heard a loud bang outside.

"What was that?", I gasped.

Gary quickly got dressed and went to go downstairs. "Stay here", he urged.

I sat there terrified by the bangs and crackles coming from downstairs, not sure what to make of it.

Seconds later Gary rushed back in and grabbed the phone. "What is it?" I demanded, I could see it was something serious.

Without answering Gary dialled 999 "The Fire Service please – I'd like to report a fire!"

Gary's beloved Volkswagen Golf was up in flames. Quickly the firemen came and put out the fire, but the car was a write-off and we were lucky we hadn't been asleep, or the barn would have soon caught fire and we would have been written-off too. The police came and took a statement. It seemed there'd been a lot of mysterious fires in the area and they asked if we had any problems with anyone. Gary explained the saga with the driveway just a few days earlier. The police thought it probably was connected, but there was nothing they could do without any evidence.

We made an insurance claim, but because he hadn't had the car long and there was a penalty for early payment, after the loan was paid, we ended up with nothing to buy another car. As it was impossible for me to get to work without one, my mum very kindly lent us her Datsun. It was green, quite old, but I enjoyed driving it. A few weeks later I was driving down a country road on my way to work in the rain. I wasn't driving that fast, but a lorry was coming the other way, so I just touched my foot on the brake to slow down. Before I knew what was happening the car had spun round, flipped over and I was left hanging by my seatbelt with the car on its side in the verge facing the opposite direction. The lorry driver had stopped and lifted me out of the broken side window (I was a lot smaller then). I shook my jumper and shards of glass sprinkled the floor, but miraculously I had not even a scratch or bruise. I was however in shock. A man who had stopped offered to drive me home. It was only ten minutes away, so I climbed into his car without a thought (not something I'd usually do) and he took me home. I can't remember much about it really; I just remember I couldn't stop shaking and feeling sick. We were once again without a car. This time, Gary's dad kindly gave us his old car – a Maxi. I really was petrified of driving again, and a Maxi with its heavy gears was not the easiest of cars to gain my confidence in, but Gary forced me to do it, despite my protestations, and I'm glad he did.

During this time there didn't seem to be a week go by without one catastrophe or another. One day we got a call from Gary's mum, his sister had been involved in quite a serious motorbike accident whilst on holiday with a friend in Ireland. A car went into the side of them on a blind junction and her leg had taken the full impact. She had fractured it in several places and was moved to a hospital in Medway where she stayed for several months. She was just nineteen (the same age as me). It was a difficult time for the whole family, and we spent most of our weekends returning to Kent to visit her and Gary's mum who was living on her own at the time.

This was not the end of our car related disasters, the most tragic of which involved the fiancé of Sally, the girl I shared an office with. I had become very friendly with her and we were invited to her engagement party. There were about sixty guests in a marquee in their garden. After a great party, we left about 11pm and were shocked to find out that not long after we left, there had been a tragic incident. Sally's fiancé John had asked some gate crashers to leave. The gate crashers didn't take kindly to this and returned later in their car and aimed straight for him. The car hit him, and he fell, hit his head on the pavement and tragically died later that night. It was a terrible shock for all of us, not least of all for poor Sally who was of course devastated.

Gary's job was not proceeding as planned either. Mrs B turned out to be a "B" in nature too. She was running out of money and got Gary to sack all the staff she'd instructed him to employ. He felt she had always intended to just employ them for a few months, and he wished she had been honest with him from the start. It wasn't nice having to lay everyone off. It was the final straw for Gary and so he quit, and we left the little flat above the barn and moved into a bedsit in Guildford town centre. It was a tiny room on the third floor with a shared bathroom. And so there we were with very little money, living in a grotty room in a busy town and struggling to cope with one traumatic experience after another. Gary managed to get a bit of part-time work at the removals company I worked for and they even offered him a full-time job, but it wasn't what he wanted to do with his life.

A new start in Kent

Eventually the catalogue of disasters took their toll and we decided to give up trying to make it work in Surrey and moved back to Kent. In the six months we had been away (yes, all that happened in only six months), my parents had bought a hotel in Folkestone, so we initially stayed in one of their guest rooms at the top of the big four storey semi-detached Victorian property. Suddenly, everything started to fall into place for us at last. I got a job at the end of the road as a secretary in the aviation department of an insurance company and Gary worked as a stock controller for a local firm. He hated it, but it paid the bills. A flat came up for sale next door and within a few months we were the proud owners of a Victorian two-bed, second floor flat. It was a mess with poo, literally up the walls in the spare room and the sitting room carpet was caked with dried in cats wee. Everything needed decorating, but it was structurally sound and had lots of potential. All our spare time and money was spent on doing it up. Gary got a weekend job putting in a large pond and rockery for a friend of a friend called Geoff. He was so impressed with Gary's work and unmistakable knowledge, that he offered to go into business with him as a silent partner in a landscape gardening company. He would provide the money and the business knowledge and Gary would provide the skills. It was an opportunity too good to miss, so Gary gave up his job as a stock controller and started "Second Nature" Landscaping. The business really took off and within a few years we had a couple of teams of landscapers.

In 1988, a year after starting the business, we got married. It was a wonderful wedding day – we married in the Folkestone Registry Office and had our photos taken in the beautiful gardens opposite. One hundred guests joined us for the reception at The Metropole Hotel which is on the cliffs overlooking the sea and all thoroughly enjoyed our day. We had our honeymoon on the Island of Zante, which at the time was very quiet and unspoilt. We had a wonderful time, and this further cemented our wish to one day move abroad.

The following year we sold our flat in Folkestone for double the price we paid for it and bought a two-bed cottage in a village on the outskirts of Faversham. On the advice of a bank manager acquaintance, we borrowed more than we needed and spent the extra money on new carpets and furniture. We loved that little beamed cottage. Gary built a conservatory from old windows, landscaped the garden and planted some beautiful trees and shrubs. All were destroyed unfortunately by our latest addition to the family – a Saint Bernard pup called Sasha. She also ruined our brand-new peach carpet with her big muddy paws and chewed our new three-piece cottage suite and my Grandfather's Ercol table and chairs. It was at this point that I realised I could never be house-proud. If I was fussy about things like that, I'd have had a nervous breakdown years ago!

Our business was blossoming, and we now had three landscaping teams. We decided it was time to start a family and I became pregnant very quickly. Soon after, Gary's partner Geoff started becoming less of a silent partner and more a very noisy one. He had sold his main business (a chain of estate agents) and was becoming more actively involved in Second Nature. Geoff was pushing for more commercial contracts, and we weren't happy with the way it was going. Gary much preferred landscaping private gardens than doing the contract turfing and small plantings of the housing estates for building firms. However, Geoff was insistent that this should be our "bread and butter" work and was actively quoting for more contracts. After a lot of talking and thinking, we concluded that we would have to break away from the partnership and go it alone. We appreciated all that Geoff had done for us, but felt it was time to go our separate ways. Breaking the news to him was one of the hardest things we've ever had to do. We liked him and his wife very much and had a lot of admiration for everything he had achieved. We didn't want to seem ungrateful, but it just wasn't working. He was obviously hurt and angry, but he took it quite well considering the circumstances.

We worked out exactly how much he had put into the business financially and we took a large loan to pay him off. Those last few months were very hard – I was pregnant and had to work in the office with Geoff every day. He was a very strong character and I had a few stand-offs with him, but he was really very fair. We kept in touch and although it was difficult initially, we did visit him several times and still exchange cards at Christmas. We will always be grateful to him and his wife for the help they gave us. As it turned out I think the break-up of the partnership proved to be the best outcome for him as none of us foresaw what was about to happen less than a year later.

Initially everything worked out fine, even though it was difficult to pay the loan on top of the mortgage, but it was doable. I worked from home seven days a week. Every evening was spent catching up with estimates and going through work schedules and orders. Gary was landscaping and managing the three teams. We had five staff, two of whom were cousins of Gary's, one of them lived with us during this period. Things were going well and to top it off our beautiful son Matthew was born in March 1990.

We worked hard trying to get to a point where we had enough money to make our dream of moving abroad a reality. Things were going well for us and we seemed to have the perfect life - a booming business, which was completely ours, we lived in a very cute cottage in a quiet village, we had a soppy St. Bernard, chickens in the garden, a beautiful baby boy and life was sweet. I was only twenty-three and already had achieved more than any of my friends, most of whom were still at university. We felt confident that in a few years we would be able to sell up and move to Greece - we even started taking Greek lessons in readiness (how useful).

But then in 1992 the UK plunged into a recession and our perfect lives started to crumble around us. Interest rates on our mortgage doubled almost overnight as did the interest on our loan. Two of our largest clients - building companies - went into liquidation not only owing us money but also cutting our income by more than half and there was nothing we could do about it. We had so many outgoings and wages, etc., we could no longer afford to cover everything. The debts started mounting, we held on as long as we could but eventually, when we didn't even have enough money to eat, we had to take the tough decision to lay off our staff. Whilst we managed to reduce staffing costs, we still had huge overheads and a potential income flow cut by two thirds. It was an impossible situation. I stopped answering the phone as I couldn't bear the constant demands for money which we couldn't pay, and I couldn't see a way out. There was no help for us from the Government – on paper we still had a good income, they wouldn't take into account that we had to pay a large mortgage and a loan, plus all the other mounting debts. We lived off handouts from kind relatives, it was a difficult time.

We decided to try and sell the house – we put it on the market, but no one was buying. We both worked so hard. When Matthew was nine months old, I had to get another job to help make ends meet. We were hoping it would only be for a few months, but it ended up being for much longer. Gary's sister looked after him for the first few months, but when she got a job, he had to go to a day nursery. It was difficult and he didn't really like it, but what choice did we have? The extra money I was earning was helping to keep the wolves from the door.

On Matthew's second birthday, he was very ill – he had bronchitis which developed into a full-blown asthma attack and he was admitted to hospital a day later. He was there for a week. I was with him most of the time, but I too was ill with tonsillitis. It was a very low point. I remember watching him in the hospital struggling to breathe and wondering what it was all about. Why were we working so hard, missing out on this little one's childhood to pay extortionate interest charges to banks and building companies. Our world had gone crazy. After Matthew came out of hospital, he continued often to be poorly. I negotiated with my work to reduce my hours to part time. This helped a little, but whenever I left to go to work, Matthew would have an asthma attack and we decided in the end that I would have to give up work to be with him. Of course, the loss of my regular wage was devastating to us, but Gary had just managed to secure a big landscaping contract – it was going to be our saviour. Unfortunately, it wasn't enough, and our business folded.

Gary then tried to look for a job. He applied for lots, but it was difficult to get a position in horticulture when he had no qualifications to prove his substantial knowledge. After a few let downs, we decided that the best solution was for him to go to university and get a degree. We knew it would be tough with a young family but felt that the sacrifices would be worth it. So, at thirty, he enrolled on a full-time course at Hadlow College and started a BSc Degree in Amenity Horticulture and Landscape Management. He worked weekends and any spare time he had doing gardening jobs or whatever else he could to help make ends meet.

We had been holding off from having any more children because of our financial situation, but in the end as Matthew turned three, we decided there was never going to be a good time, so in March 1994 Ryan was born.

When I first became pregnant with Ryan, we still had our little cottage, payments on the mortgage had resumed, the house was on the market, but we had a lot of arrears and the mortgage company took us to court. We were hoping that the court would find in our favour and allow us to stay in the house until we sold it to pay off the debt. The court case was three weeks before Ryan was born and so I arrived at the Court House heavily pregnant and highly emotional. Unfortunately, despite our pleas, the case did not go our way and a repossession order was granted. I was inconsolable and so once again fate had dealt us a hard blow and three months after Ryan was born, we found ourselves homeless. As we had young children, the council housed us in temporary accommodation while we were waiting for a council house to become available. It was a purpose-built block of flats in a not particularly pleasant area. We were grateful for a roof over our heads, but it was grim. Very noisy with people knocking on our door or window at all times of day and night asking if we wanted to buy yesterday's paper or if we could spare a cigarette. We kept our heads down and tried not to make eye contact with anyone and luckily, six weeks later we were offered a two-bed house on a small housing association estate of about thirty houses in a lovely little village not far from my hometown.

As we pulled up to move into our new home, we were greeted by next door's three-year-old raising her middle finger to her eight-year-old brother shouting "F*** off you c***". A charming welcome to the neighbourhood! However, despite the family next door, the family on the other side became firm friends as did many other people on the estate. We had some tough times but also have some happy memories during our six years there.

We were lucky in our unluckiness. The village school was nice and was in a lovely rural area. The boys could play outside safely which was good. Although there was that one time when four-year-old Ryan was playing on his tricycle and got blocked by Craig the bully from next door who was seven years older than him. When Ryan came home in tears, I saw red and marched up to Craig shouting at him in front of all his friends.

"What do you think you are doing bullying a little boy more than half your age? Are you proud of yourself? LOOK AT ME WHEN I'M TALKING TO YOU!" I screamed. Everyone stopped and stared at this woman, who was normally so quiet and shy and didn't say a word.

"Don't you EVER go near my son again, do you understand?"

There was no response from wide eyed Craig.

"DO YOU UNDERSTAND!" I bellowed in his face. He nodded sheepishly and thankfully never went near Ryan again.

Climbing back up

We spent the rest of the nineties, retraining and working hard to get back to where we had been before the recession. Gary studied full time and worked in his spare time doing gardening jobs to make ends meet. I took on part-time work too, typing from home during the week while the children were small. I even got a weekend job; I was one of those annoying people at Superstore exits trying to badger you into an appointment for double glazing. You think that sounds bad? Well, Gary had an evening job testing dog wee at the local Racetrack. Yes, someone actually has to do that! Once the boys were both at school, I was able to get a better job and I started working part-time on an IT help desk whilst studying for a Certificate in Education.

Our lives were beginning to improve. In 1997 Gary finished his BSc and was offered a position as a Horticultural Lecturer at the college he studied at and I qualified and started working as an IT trainer, we moved about six doors up to a three bed house on the same estate and things were starting to ease up financially. We both had good jobs, the boys were happy at school and doing well.

We had worked hard to get into a position to get back on the property ladder and had an opportunity to buy my parents guest house on the Kent coast. It was slightly run down as they were close to retirement and had been considering selling or turning the house into flats. We took on the challenge and spent the next three years continuing with part-time jobs and running, renovating and developing the guest house at the same time. It wasn't easy and we had no social life, but we were determined to make a better life for ourselves and our children. Thoughts of moving abroad had been pushed to the background. We decided it was difficult to move Matthew and Ryan when they were settled, so perhaps it would be better to wait until they had both left home. However, life was about to tempt us in another direction.

In 2002 we welcomed our third son James into the world - Mathew and Ryan were twelve and eight. I had intended to go back to work a few months after the birth (I was working part-time as IT support for the local probation office), but we very soon discovered that that wouldn't be possible. James was not the easiest of children. In fact, we called him 'the screamer'! He never slept soundly during the night until he was three years old and would often scream for no apparent reason during the day. We put it down to him having been induced two weeks early. I had been very poorly during the second half of the pregnancy and we had been told that there was a risk of him being stillborn if they didn't induce the birth. It was quite evident he was happy in the womb and wasn't ready to come out. He screamed from the moment he took his first breath. When he wasn't screaming, he was sleeping with his eyes tightly shut and brow furrowed, as if he was trying to block out the world he had been so rudely dragged into before he was ready.

It was during the first year of James' life that we started to think we really couldn't wait another eighteen or so years until James left home before we moved abroad. At the same time the value of our property had significantly increased to the extent that we had enough equity to afford a sizable property without a mortgage abroad. We could have perhaps waited another year or so and gained more money as the property prices were soaring at quite a pace, but we had learnt from our experiences in the nineties that equally the market could crash and our equity could just as easily disappear. We decided that it was a case of now or never. We weren't happy with the way things were going in England, the crime, the youth culture, the politics. We felt as though we were stagnating and needed a new way of life - life is too short, and we weren't making the most of it. It was at last time to act and make our dreams a reality.

We started looking into places we might live. Greece had always been our intended new home and of all the Greek islands we had visited over the years, Crete was our first choice, as we felt it was big enough to give us the variety we needed as a family. We started looking into the practicalities of the move. Our main problem was finding a suitable school for Matthew. Ryan was still at primary school at the time and so we felt that he would be okay to go to a local Greek school as he would have the time to master the language before starting secondary school. Matthew however, aged thirteen/fourteen was at a very difficult age to move. Crete had an international school, but it was only for primary aged children. At the time Matthew was a day pupil at a local private school - he had won an academic scholarship to go there and was doing really well. It seemed wrong to move him at such a vulnerable age. We decided that perhaps the best solution was for him to remain at the same school and board. He already knew everyone there, so it would be a fairly smooth transition.

We then researched the logistics of him flying home for holidays and hit a barrier because there were no direct flights to Crete in the winter. He would have to fly to Athens and then catch a boat to Crete. This was out of the question; he was too young to be making that sort of journey and so we came to a dead end. Greece was an impractical option for us as a family and perhaps in light of their subsequent economic problems it was fortunate that we decided against it. However, we didn't give up on our idea of emigrating and the search was now on for alternative countries closer to home.

Let's move abroad, but where?

The decision to move abroad was one thing, but after discovering that Crete was a non-starter, it was more difficult choosing another country.

The choice to move to France was a gradual one. It wasn't a sudden dawning or a "eureka" moment. It happened over the course of a few months, without us being fully aware. Gary started researching suitable countries to move to on the Internet - it was his hobby. We often joked about what he would do with his evenings if we ever managed to make the move. I think perhaps "research" suggests that there was something scientific about it, but in reality, it was more about the price and the property – that was Gary's job. Then, once he found the properties he liked at prices we could afford, it was my turn to research the viability of the country – schools, health service, transport links, etc., all the boring, practical stuff. He surfed the world in the space of a few weeks. You name it, he'd googled it - from Australia to Zante.

Many of the places he considered weren't practical. He spent quite a few days looking at property in Croatia and Bulgaria, which although very cheap and may have been a good investment (as prices have increased significantly there now), they were not, I felt, places suitable for an expat family to settle permanently.

We were looking for a country with Mediterranean style weather and a slower pace of life, where we could experience and share the simple pleasures with our children. Somewhere they could grow up playing outside, exploring, free from harm. A place where they would not feel pressured by material possessions such as designer clothes and the latest video games, where drugs and crime rates were lower than they were in the UK. We wanted to find somewhere the locals were more people than possession-orientated, where family life was celebrated and encouraged rather than children seen as inconveniences that need to be 'catered' for. But, not only did our adopted country need to have all these qualities, it also had to have good transport links with the UK, a good standard of education and an adequate health service. So not a lot really!

It had to be somewhere in Europe and it really boiled down to Italy, France or Spain. We weren't keen on Spain (although we have since found some lovely parts of Northern Spain where we would consider living). Our impression of Southern Spain was that it was too touristy for us and our experiences with the Spanish people in general had not been positive ones. Also, there had been several scary reports of archaic property laws where people had lost their houses or had roads built through them, etc. Crime rates too were very high in many parts. Italy was a bit of an unknown entity; I had never been there. Gary spent two weeks there as a teenager and although he loved it, he didn't feel drawn to living there. Also, it has the reputation of being a notoriously corrupt society.

Everything seemed to be pointing towards our closest neighbour, France and Gary started exploring property there. Every now and then he'd get excited and would show me some interesting watermill, mansion or chateau in an idyllic setting for the price of a two bed semi in Kent and gradually we started to think that maybe the South of France could be a contender. Up until then, we had only done day and short trips to the north of France, and this area didn't greatly appeal to us, but properties looked very interesting in the Southwest and so we thought it would be worth it to check them out. Of course, you can only find out so much on the Internet and useful as it is, the only way you can really know what a country is like is to visit and experience it. We decided we had to go and visit Southern France and see if it was somewhere we could picture ourselves living.

First taste of France

On Gary's virtual tours of France, he had whittled down the area of most interest to the Southwest of France. We wanted to be as far south as possible – assuming that the weather would be better further south. The prices in the smart south east (Provence and the Cote d'Azur) were prohibitive, so the rural Southwest looked like a good place to start.

France is split into thirteen administrative regions and each region is divided into several departments each of which is conveniently numbered (in alphabetical order).

There are two regions that cover the Southwest quarter of France, which we were considering, the region of Occitanie (thirteen departments) and Nouvelle-Aquitaine (twelve departments).

We concentrated our search during our first visit in and around the department of Aude in the region of Occitanie (which was Languedoc-Roussillon at the time) and has Carcassonne as its capital. The A61 motorway crosses the middle of the department which links Toulouse, through Carcassonne and across to Narbonne on the Mediterranean coast. It's well situated for airports being within easy access to Toulouse and there is also an international airport at Carcassonne with direct flights to many parts of the UK with budget airlines like Ryanair. If I had any criticism of the area it would be the wind – it's well known that this is one of the windiest parts of France, being affected by the "tramontane" and the "mistral" (strong, dry, cold winds from the north or northwest, respectively). Many of the trees grow on a slant due to the wind, which blows between three hundred and three hundred and fifty days a year!

For our first visit we booked a week in a *gîte* in a small village near Carcassonne. *Gîte* is the word the French use to describe a property used for short-term rental. Traditionally a *gîte* was perhaps a small house or apartment with basic facilities let by farmers to generate a bit of extra income. Nowadays, *gîtes* come in all shapes and sizes from the very basic to the very luxurious. This particular *gîte* was a newly renovated village house with two bedrooms and all the basic necessities for a holiday. It was situated in a quaint little village at the top of a hill, as many of the villages are in this part of France. We arrived at night and settled the children down to sleep. Matthew (thirteen) and Ryan (nine) shared the attic room and James was sleeping in a travel cot set up in our room. He was nearly twelve months old – in fact we celebrated his first birthday and he took his first steps in that very *gîte*. In the morning we awoke to blazing sunshine streaming through our bedroom window, a chink of deep blue sky just visible through the gap in the curtains. Gary jumped out of bed and threw the windows open.

"Wow, look at that view Nicks". We were surprised to find that the Pyrenees could be seen in the distance – it was not something we had expected. "I'm liking it already", he beamed. It was a good start.

We spent the week exploring. We had a few properties lined up to view, but this visit was really more about seeing if we felt that France was somewhere we could live and what type of properties were available in our budget. What surprised us most about the area was how Mediterranean it felt – obviously the sunshine helped, but it was also full of quaint little villages with winding roads and beautiful farm cottages and stone-built houses with blue shutters. The countryside was dotted with Italian cypress growing by the roadside. It was certainly nothing like some of the dreary places we had visited in the north.

Most people associate France with its cuisine and whilst we couldn't really test out any fine dining restaurants, we were impressed with the general quality of the food. The lunchtime meal is the most important meal of the day. A two-hour lunch break to enjoy a three-course meal is the norm. We found it strange to begin with, as we were so used to just grabbing a sandwich and carrying on. All shops close for at least two hours and their lunchtime meal is between 12 and 2pm. If you get to a restaurant after 1:30pm you are likely to be disappointed, as there will either be nothing left, or they won't serve you. This was difficult to start with as we were so used to eating whenever we felt like it. We discovered quite quickly that you must be organised about food in France or you'll go hungry (not a good idea with young children in tow).

Most restaurants offer a *Plat du jour* which is the main dish (or dishes) of the day. Back in 2003/4 when we were searching for our new home the *Menu du jour* cost between 8 and 12 euros a head and today remains keenly priced. It usually comprises of an entrée (maybe a soup or a buffet of cold meats and salads), followed by the *Plat du jour*, a dessert and often a ¼ litre of wine included in the price. The restaurants are filled at lunchtime with local workers having a hearty meal washed down with a couple of glasses of red wine. We were always ready for a sleep after such a big lunch – how anyone could go back to work after, I'll never know! You can always judge the quality of the food in a restaurant by the number of cars, trucks and lorries outside at lunchtime. We found the restaurants very laid-back – welcoming families with children (which is not always the case in the UK). The local restaurant had one of their regulars sat in the dining room with his dog – which was surprising to me at the time. We didn't have a problem with it because we love dogs, but we were so conditioned by what is considered acceptable in the UK. It was refreshing to find that the French in this area were much more relaxed about things like that.

I can remember our first visit to a local market. There's something very special about a French market as the whole ethos is totally different to the British equivalent. In England we tend to associate market with "cheap". We go to the market to get a bargain – to get cheaper clothes and food. In France it's all about quality and variety. There's nothing "cheap" about a French market and if there was the French wouldn't go. As we wandered up and down looking at the stalls all spread around the village square, we saw a fascinating range of products on sale – fresh vegetables as you'd expect, but stalls filled with olives and spices of all varieties and colours; little old French men wearing their traditional berets (yes they really do, it's not just a stereotype), selling *Cèpes* (a type of wild mushroom), onions and garlic and other home grown vegetables; stalls with a wonderful wide range of saucissons (cured sausage) hanging and large hams; bread stalls brimming with *baguettes*, *flutes* (a larger baguette), *croissants*, *pains au chocolat* and *pains au raisin*, refrigerated vans selling a vast array of cheeses; stalls with olive oil and of course the wine. In many of the markets you can find a stall selling wine from the barrel and back in 2003/4 it was 80 cents a litre. We thought it must be very poor quality at that price, but it was actually very drinkable. You can tell that by the amount of French queueing up with their empty containers to buy it. We've been told that wine growers are given a certain quota of litres they are permitted to produce. If they have a glut, they sell the extra at the markets because they are not allowed to bottle it. So, it's not only just as good as the bottled stuff, it's just the same. It's good table wine but doesn't keep well (not that we often find that a problem).

All the French people we met were very friendly and relaxed, the scenery was fantastic, the food was good - we were starting to warm up to the French way of life.

One of the first properties we viewed was a hilltop château. It was in a lovely location with beautiful views across rolling lush green countryside. The château was accessed via two large gates and the building was set in a horseshoe around a courtyard with four square towers at each corner joining the building together. It was being used as a children's centre, so part of the building was habitable but organised as a school and it felt very institutional. Three quarters of it needed total renovation, but it was in such a beautiful setting and would certainly have lent itself to some sort of business. It was huge and we couldn't believe that it was so close in price to our budget. In England we would never, in our wildest dreams, have been able to buy anything like that. We knew it was a non-starter because it was at the top end of our budget and we'd have had nothing left to renovate with, but we were amazed at the size of property we could afford to buy here. It was an excellent start and filled us with hope that we would be able to find something very special in our price range.

We spent a day in the department capital of Carcassonne. It is a lovely medieval city full of history and beautiful buildings and was used in some shots in the film "Robin Hood Prince of Thieves". It was very touristy, but nevertheless well worth a visit. I later went on to read the novel "Labyrinth" by Kate Mosse, which is the first in a series of period time slip books, set in the former Languedoc Region, in and around Carcassonne and really helps to bring the history of the area alive. This area is also known as Cathar country because it was the main stronghold in the twelfth century for a form of Christianity and has the remains of many Cathar castles as a reminder of its history. The Cathars (or Les Bonnes Hommes as they called themselves) were regarded as heretics and the Catholic Church eventually started a crusade against them. One of the most remarkable aspects of the Cathars were their castles – always built at the top of a mountain or high peak in very inaccessible locations. How did they get the stones up there to build them? During the Crusades, when under attack, the Cathars would retreat to their castles and could be under siege for months. One of the last strongholds and most famous of the Cathar castles is Montségur in the Ariège. The Cathars were held under siege for ten months before finally surrendering and subsequently being burnt to death.

We visited a Cathar castle in Quéribus and were very impressed. The scenery was spectacular through the winding roads of the Pyrenees – it was a really clear day and the mountains looked magnificent. When we arrived, we parked in the village at the bottom and could see the remains of the castle perched high at the top of a hill above us. It was quite a climb over rock and uneven steps and paths to get to the top, which I hadn't been prepared for. I cursed myself for stupidly wearing flip-flops as I looked with envy at the other climbers with their sensible shoes. Flip-flops aside, it wasn't an easy climb with two daring boys and a toddler. James was only one, so we had to take turns carrying him while Matthew and Ryan kept running on ahead. It was our first experience facing the lack of safety regulations in public places in France. There were literally sheer drops with no barriers, easily accessible to anyone and it was a nightmare

28

climbing up there with two very inquisitive and active boys. It even unnerved Gary to see the boys fooling about on the edge of a precipice – and it takes a lot to get him panicked! When we got to the top though, it was worth the effort. The views were fantastic, no wonder the Cathars chose this spot – not only was it beautiful, but they would be able to see their enemies coming from miles away.

We were really enjoying our stay and were impressed with what we had seen. We were coming around to the thought that this could really be a part of the world in which we could settle and enjoy bringing up our children. We started looking more seriously at the property in the area with a view to a permanent move. Transport links were excellent to the UK, the education system seemed sound, the weather was much better, the scenery was fantastic, the people were friendly, the food was great, the wine even better, what more could we want?

Towards the end of our visit, we viewed a property near Revel on the border in the Haute-Garonne (about 60km north west of Carcassonne) near lac de Saint-Ferréol - it was a rambling old farmhouse with lots of land and a sizable lake. The house was very large, a bit shabby and full of stuffed animals. Deer heads, foxes and pheasants watched our every move which was very off-putting, but despite that we could see some potential in the property. The owner was not only a killer of badgers but also a bit of a "bodger". He had devised a heating system using large exposed silver coiled piping, which crossed like a series of spaghetti junctions over every room in the house. Having lived through several very cold winters here now I can sort of understand that sometimes, the necessity for warmth outweighs aesthetics, but this was more than even I could bear. It would need to be ripped out and the whole house totally redecorated and a new (aesthetically pleasing) heating system installed, but that wasn't difficult. The price was good, and we would have enough money left over to make the property really nice. One thing you need to have when viewing property in any country is vision. Luckily Gary and I have it in abundance, in fact sometimes we're so busy visualising what a property could look like that we overlook what it is in reality.

Our holiday was coming to a close and we had some decisions to make. We decided that yes, we were ready to make the move and whilst it wasn't our first choice, the Southwest of France was the place most suited for us at this stage in our lives, so the property in Revel became our goal and our journey towards our new life abroad had begun.

Screaming through France

The search for our new home had begun in earnest. The house in Revel became the benchmark for all other properties – we watched it almost daily on the Internet to make sure it was still for sale. Over the next year we spent every "holiday" and several short breaks in different parts of Southwest France to get a feel for where we would like to live and also to help us formulate our criteria for the type of property we wanted to live in. It wasn't easy for any of us. It sounds exciting scouring the French countryside for the ideal home, but the reality was very different. It wasn't the children's idea of fun driving for hours to look at one house after another. It wouldn't have been so bad if it hadn't been for James, who at twelve months old was too young to understand what was going on. He didn't travel well (he was not the easiest of children) and he literally screamed his way through France! Matthew and Ryan would take turns watching him while we viewed various properties. Neither of them particularly enjoyed it as it wasn't an easy task! We tried to intersperse fun days between house-viewing days, but it couldn't really be classed as a true holiday. Nevertheless, house hunt we did and despite the difficulties, we managed to formulate our criteria with every house we visited.

For our next trip (or should I say trial) we took a two-week holiday and decided to spend one week in the north of the Nouvelle-Aquitaine Region and the second week in the north of Occitanie. The area we were focusing on used to be called the "Limousin" and we noticed that the properties there were generally cheaper and whilst it was further north than where we had looked before, we wanted to see how the two areas compared. When we arrived at the Limoges airport, we went to pick up our hire car, a five door Renault. Try as we might we could not fit in all our baggage and bulky pushchair – it's amazing how much paraphernalia you need to cart around when you have babies and toddlers. After several attempts at packing and unpacking the car, we eventually had to give in and admit it just wasn't going to fit – it must have looked very funny to any onlookers! Finally beaten, we all traipsed back to the car hire desk.

"Sorry, we can't fit all our luggage in – we need a bigger car" Gary explained in a mixture of French and English.

The girl at the desk looked at us blankly "Sorry, there are no other cars available".

"Well, you'll have to give us a refund and we'll go to another company because we can't fit in all our luggage – it's just not possible, we've tried". With that she swiftly picked up the phone and started dialling another site. Our command of the French language at the time wasn't great, but we could pick out the odd word and understand the gist of what she was saying (well I could anyway). At one point during the telephone conversation she mentioned "Limousin" at which Gary interrupted with "No, no, we don't need a limousine - an estate car will do!" The girl behind the counter looked at him in astonishment. I found it difficult to stop myself from laughing and explained that she was talking about "Limousin" the area and wasn't ordering us a luxury car! Eventually, they found us a bigger car (a Kangoo I think it was, so not a limousine) and luggage packed, kids strapped in, we set off to find our accommodation.

The former Limousin region (now in the northern part of Nouvelle-Aquitaine) is situated in south-central France. It included the departments of Coreze, Creuse and Haute-Vienne. It's an area full of lakes and rivers and is very green and lush. It's one of the least populated areas of France, which is something you need to think carefully about if moving here with a young family. We were heading for Marvel in Haute-Vienne where we'd booked a week in a chalet beside a lake. The site was rather tucked away, but thankfully was well sign-posted or we might never have found it. It was a lovely drive through pretty countryside – very green and leafy. We travelled for some time along winding country lanes with branches overhanging the roads forming a tunnel of trees. We realised we hadn't passed any houses for some time and were hoping we were still going in the right direction. We finally descended a fairly steep hill and right at the bottom was a sharp turn to the left, then it suddenly opened out into a clearing and we had arrived.

It was a beautiful spot and just the type of property we were looking for (but way over our budget). The main building was a traditional seventeenth century stone farmhouse set at the bottom of a twenty-five-acre wooded valley with a large lake. The farmhouse had bed and breakfast facilities and a restaurant and there were several self-catering chalets. We were staying in a two-bed chalet overlooking the lake – it was perfect. Gary was in his element as he loves to fish, and to be able to do so in the evenings while the kids were sleeping was his idea of heaven. We got our things unpacked, had a cup of tea, freshened up and then headed over to the restaurant for our evening meal.

The owners were a friendly English couple and they and their parents were more than happy to share their experiences of living in France with us. This was their first season and so they were still learning the ropes themselves. They told us about the abundance of wildlife and birds in the area, which is one thing we had already noticed on the drive down. They also revealed that the house had been a hideout for the French Resistance during the Second World War – this was not surprising as it was so tucked away and hidden from view. Unfortunately, though, the Germans had somehow discovered the hideout (a tip off, I would imagine) and everyone found there had been rounded up outside the house and shot. It was a sad reminder of France's not so distant past. Not far from here was the village of Oradour-sur-Glane. The original village still stands as a memorial to the day, Saturday 10th June 1944, when German troops marched into the village and brutally murdered over six hundred men, women and children before destroying much of the village. It seems so sad that such a beautiful and peaceful place should have such a painful history.

We arranged to view a property we had been eyeing on the Internet. The pictures looked fantastic – there was a very large country house with beautiful gardens and a tennis court. We could see it needed some updating, but even so, it seemed very reasonable for the price and would leave us money over for renovations. We had arranged to meet the agent in a town not far from where we were staying. In France it seems that it is always the agent who will meet you and show you a house, rarely the owners. They often take you in their car to view properties, but as there were five of us, this wasn't possible, so we followed him in our car. It was a long drive, almost an hour away from where we were staying, and the children were getting very restless. James had started screaming as usual and we were trying to distract him by pointing out all the animals on the way and teaching him the sounds they make. "Oh, look James, there's a cow, what sound does a cow make?", "Moo", James would dutifully reply, you know the sort of thing. Matthew decided it would be amusing to teach him the sound of an old French man, so whenever we saw an old man with a beret on, he would point him out to James and say "What does an old man say James?", "Mehhhh", would come the nasal reply, followed by giggles. "Matthew, I'm not sure you should be teaching him that!" I scolded, but I must admit it kept them all amused.

We were surprised by the lack of people around. Often, we would drive through villages and not see a single soul (bar the odd old French man) – where was everyone? It didn't seem to matter at what time of day we passed through, there was not much sign of life. As the journey was nearing its end, we were in an area where there were lots of pylons crossing the road and as we turned off the main road, I noticed a sign for the village we were looking for, so realised we must be nearly there. On our right-hand side, we passed an electricity substation, which was a very ugly mass of pylons and cables. "Uh-oh, this isn't looking very promising", observed Gary. As we drew up at the house, we could instantly see the reason the house was so cheap. It had a huge electrical pylon carrying high voltage cables crossing directly in front of the house and across the property. I wouldn't even get out the car. What was the point of viewing the house, there was no way I would live there with the children. We were cross with the agent for not telling us, he was very apologetic and said it was his first viewing too and he didn't know about the pylon. We didn't view any more properties with that agent.

Whilst staying in this area, we also visited the neighbouring Departments of Charante and Charante-Maritime. We viewed a watermill in Charente-Maritime and found the drive from Limoges through to Charente a little dull. The countryside was very flat and open, and you could see for miles. It was noticeably drier than the Limousin area and had a very different feel to it. Charente-Maritime is noted for its micro-climate and has good summers and mild winters and there was certainly more happening there. It's the second most highly populated department in France, so if it's weather and people you're looking for, then it's certainly worth considering. Of course, it's also a department bordered on the west side by the Atlantic Ocean, so you would never be far from the sea. The watermill we looked at, whilst a nice building, was in an area too built up for us and it no longer had any water running to it. It had very little land and was in the middle of a town, not far from Royan. A very nice town, but we were looking for something more rural. We were surprised at how busy Royan is – it's a very large, smart and bustling town on the coast. I can see the area's appeal and I think probably from a business point of view it would be a good place to settle, but it wasn't exactly what we were looking for. We had set our sights on something more rural and relaxed.

We visited a few properties in the Nouvelle-Aquitaine region. One of these properties was an old watermill in the Pyrénées-Atlantiques. As the name would suggest, the southern half of the department is in the Pyrenees and the northern half is on the edge of the Pyrenees. The agent wasn't keen to show us the property as he'd had people in the past just drive past and refuse to view as it looked very tired and needed a lot of work. However, we are not faint-hearted and always up for a challenge, so we insisted on viewing it. The house was sound but needed a lot of work – it would be big enough for us, but not big enough for guest accommodation too. We started toying with the idea of putting log cabins in the grounds and the possibility of reintroducing a canal from the river (which no longer ran to the watermill). We arranged to meet the *Maire* (mayor) to discuss our plans and see if he had any objections.

The *Maire* is an important figure in the French system and they have a much greater role in the community than their British equivalent. Every town and village has a *Maire* and the place to meet him (or her) is in the *Mairie* or *Hotel de Ville* (town hall), which are often quite surprisingly elaborate buildings, even in small villages in the middle of nowhere with no shops! So, Gary went with Matthew (who spoke a little French) and the English estate agent met with the local *Maire*, while I stayed behind with the others. The meeting went well, and he seemed very happy that we were taking an interest in the property, he could see no problems with the ideas we had. We decided to make an offer, only to be told that the owners had decided to up the asking price. Suddenly it appeared that although the property had been on the market for ages with no interest, because we had started to get enthusiastic about it and voice our ideas, the owners had decided it was worth more! We were sorry but no, it wasn't worth more to us as it would have cost a lot of money to implement the plans we had for it. So, we left without a backward glance!

Whilst exploring the Nouvelle-Aquitaine region, we visited the department of the Landes. This area is a very flat coastal department noted for its pine forests, which were apparently planted in the early nineteenth century to prevent the erosion of the department's sandy soil by the sea. The combination of sandy soil and pine forests have created an excellent acid soil (good for growing Rhododendrons and Camellias) and much of the *terre de bruyère* or ericaceous (acid) compost supplied throughout France originates from here. We viewed another watermill in Dax. Gary was very taken with it, but I thought it was too small for a start and just didn't get a good vibe from it. It's funny how sometimes you get an instinctive feeling about a place when you're property hunting – it just doesn't feel right. Shortly after I had a dream that the lake on the land just beyond the house overflowed and flooded the house, so there was no way I was even going to contemplate that one!

We thought we'd look at a couple of properties in the Dordogne as it was only just over the border. We could see why it's so popular with the British. The Dordogne is often known as Dordogneshire or "Little Britain" due to the large numbers of expats living or owning second homes there. It really is very pretty and is often described as Britain 50 years ago. We liked the properties we saw, but nothing seemed quite right for us as the prices made them just a little out of our reach.

On returning to the Limousin area we decided we really liked it there and it was during this visit that we found a lovely slate roofed watermill (*moulin*) in the Creuse. It was a big house, which could be easily split into two and had another smaller house for renovation. It had a lot of land (mainly woodland), which was really pretty and had a working turbine generating a small amount of electricity from the stream running through the property. I could imagine living there and could visualise all the improvements we could make to the house. The children weren't quite as enthusiastic, they thought the grey slate roof gave the building a depressing appearance. I was sure I could win them round though if we were to make an offer. However, we decided to wait and see what we thought of the properties we were due to view in our second week. On reflection, we decided that whilst the Creuse was very picturesque, it was a little too remote for us as a family. Also, the weather wouldn't suit us, being hot in the summer, with very wet and cold winters. We really wanted to have Mediterranean weather with a few more neighbours, so we moved our search further south.

Discovering our new home

We next decided to explore the Occitanie region a little further, an area that was formerly called the "Midi Pyrenees" (and still is by many which is very confusing for newcomers). We spent a week in northern Gers, in a *bastide* town called Montreal du Gers near Condom (yes, a rather unfortunate name I know – you can imagine what our sons thought about the prospect of living there!). *Bastides* are fortified towns which date back to around the 12th century. Many of the *bastide* towns have medieval style buildings with arcades around a central square. They are very attractive towns and are typically found in this region.

We were staying in a quaint stone-built village house just around the corner from the main central square. On our first evening we found a little bar/restaurant open in the square which was quite lively and very friendly, where we had our first taste of "*Floc de Gascogne*" which is an aperitif made from wine fortified with Armagnac (another speciality of this region). We became very fond of it and I know it is supposed to be drunk as an aperitif, but one glass just led to another one and the bottle didn't last very long! We also had our first taste of *confit de canard*, which originates from here too. This is a delicious recipe of duck legs preserved with salt, herbs and spices and then cooked in duck fat, often served with French beans in garlic and sauté potatoes.

We liked the area and looked at lots of possible properties. One in particular captured our imagination – it was a farmhouse near Nogaro with several outbuildings which could be converted into holiday accommodation, but the real winning element, for Gary in particular, was that it had two hectares of vines and a further ten hectares of land. It was a nice property with loads of potential and very reasonably priced. It had a gated entrance and a long driveway leading up to a group of buildings arranged in a horseshoe around a courtyard.

The main house had been recently renovated and was a bit modern for my liking, but we could always change it. It had an enclosed garden at the back, which would be ideal for the children, and an established fenced vegetable garden or *potager*. To the right of the house were the remains of an old stone building - most of the walls were still intact but the roof was missing. It was a real suntrap and I had visions of making it a terrace by paving the floor, putting a table and chairs there and growing climbers and vines on the walls. It was full of character and I could just imagine us sitting there on a summer's evening, sipping a glass of wine and looking over the vineyard laid out before us. The horseshoe of buildings included a couple of open barns full of old farm machinery separated by a big double gateway in the centre of the horseshoe, which opened out onto the back. Next to this was a small *colombage* house which could be easily renovated to make a very nice two bed-roomed *gîte*.

We both really loved the property - it was so tempting that we decided to make an offer (even though we hadn't sold our own property at the time). Before we had left England on this trip, we had had someone really interested in the guest house and so were fairly confident we'd get a buyer soon. We were over the moon when our offer was accepted, but it then had to go through *SAFER* (*Société d'Aménagement Foncier et d'Etablissement Rural*), which is a government agency. Any property sales that include agricultural land, must go through them, and they have first option to buy the property. After several weeks of waiting we were told that the sale was not legal - the owners had been given a government grant to renovate the house, to offer it as cheap rental accommodation to farm workers. If they sold the property within ten years of the grant, they would be liable to pay back the money, so they withdrew the property from the market and that particular dream was brought to an abrupt end.

On our next visit we stayed in a house near Plaisance, which is further south in the Gers. During this trip, we celebrated James' second birthday, which also marked the first anniversary of our hunt for our new home in France. The house was owned by an English musician called George, who divided his time between his home in the Gers and visiting his girlfriend in Paris. When he wasn't at the house, he let it to holiday makers and house hunters like us. He was off to Paris the next day, but for the first night of our trip he stayed in a campervan he kept in the garden. He had a drum kit in the house - much to Matthew's delight as he was learning to play the drums and George taught him about syncopated rhythm. He offered the children a drink - he had some *cassis* which James drank with some relish. We had thought it was a soft drink used as a mixer, but later found that it was *Crème de Cassis* which is actually a liqueur made from blackcurrants. He slept well that night!

George told us about the Marciac jazz festival which is held in the Gers every July/August. It's very famous and he was always fully booked during that period as his house was only thirty minutes away from the festival. Marciac is a lovely *bastide* town to visit at any time, but it is particularly lovely on a summer's afternoon during the jazz festival. I went along there once a few years later when Matthew had a friend visiting. The town is closed off to traffic for the festival with plenty of organised parking on the outskirts of the town. A stage is set up in the central square with seating, bars and food available all around. You can stop and listen to the bands and it's all free. Just outside the main square is the marquee for the main events which are big jazz names who perform in the evening, but you have to book and pay for those. The rest of the festival is completely free, and it has a lovely relaxed atmosphere. There are also lots of stalls selling various things and street entertainers for the children. The festival has grown over the years and it attracts famous names from across the world - this year for example Sting, Gregory Porter, George Benson and the Jacksons. Last year Joan Baez and Carlos Santana. As well as the marquee (*chapiteau*) which holds 6,000 and hosts the biggest names, there's also a range of other venues including L'Astrada, a new auditorium built in 2011 which offers concerts throughout the year.

During this visit we viewed a château in Saint-Béat which is in Haute-Garonne. The department covers a large area including Toulouse (which is also the capital of the Occitanie region) to the north and then stretches right down to Luchon and Saint-Béat in the Pyrenees on the Spanish border. As we pulled up outside and stood talking to the agent, two vultures were circling in the mountains high above us. This was our first viewing with Frans, a clean-cut (at that time) Flemish estate agent – he turned out later on to play a significant role in our move to France. Estate agents in France are very different to those in the UK. The biggest difference is the size of their commission - usually between 5-10%! However, in their defence it is an expensive business being an estate agent in France. They all seem to work only on a commission basis and have to travel long distances to show houses – often to people on holiday with no real intention of moving to France. They usually spend the entire day (or several days) showing clients around various properties and this can often be for nothing. That's without the cost of their *cotisations* - which is the French equivalent of National Insurance and is a compulsory which can amount to as much as 45% of your yearly earnings as a self-employed person (and that's before taxes!). They also often offer other services like helping you get started when you arrive (sorting out insurance, getting services connected, etc.). It's important to have a good relationship with your estate agent as he/she can prove to be an invaluable help through the buying process and beyond.

We loved the *château*, it was beautiful with lots of its original decorative ceilings, panelled walls and very high ceilings and doors. It had an outbuilding and there was also a river running though the garden. Perfect, but it was right at the top end of our budget. We wouldn't have had any money left to renovate it and it needed a new roof. Had the roof been sound we may have considered it, as it really was a lovely property. Now with the benefit of hindsight and having lived in the region for some time, I'm glad we didn't choose to live there. I prefer to live within an hour's drive of the Pyrenees as I love having them in the background. When you live in the mountains you can't see the beauty of them so clearly and it's quite a bleak place in the winter.

By now we had a pretty clear idea of the property we wanted. Our criteria were:

1. Big enough to accommodate us and have further holiday letting possibilities
2. Within an hour's drive to an airport with direct links to the UK
3. Preferably with a fishing lake or river
4. In the countryside, but not too remote
5. Views of the Pyrenees would be nice but not essential
6. Some renovation work OK, but not a complete rebuild
7. Rural, but within easy distance of all amenities (shops, schools, etc.)
8. At least a hectare of land
9. Within easy reach of Spain and the mountains

It was about this time that Gary came across a watermill advertised on the Internet in the Haute-Garonne. "What do you think of this one?" he asked me enthusiastically. "It's a watermill, it's big, it's got land, it's within an hour of Toulouse, it's got a lake – it meets all our criteria".

"You must be joking!" He showed me a picture of what looked like a very ugly factory building – it was huge about three or four stories high and the façade was a mixture of crumbling stone, render and red brick. There was no way I was even going to look at that one!

A few weeks later, Ryan found the same watermill on the internet, but with another agency which gave maybe fifty photos of all the land included in the sale, inside the property and a picture of the property from a distance with its reflection in the lake. This time, after seeing how beautiful the land around it was including a lake and river, waterfalls, woodland, outbuildings and how much potential it had inside with lots of rooms already partially renovated - I was starting to warm to the property. It was certainly unusual and had "huge" potential (huge being the operative word!) It was so big we could do whatever we liked with it. We decided it was definitely worth viewing and we added it to our list for our next trip. We contacted Frans who was the agent again, and he sent us copies of the floor plans, which really helped us visualise the layout inside. Unfortunately, though, during our next trip we couldn't view it as it was under offer. So that was that, or so we thought.

Moulin d'en Bas 2003

Shortly after returning to the UK and about a year after putting our property on the market, we finally had a serious buyer for our guest house, but we had no property to go to. The sensible thing to do would be to rent in the area we were interested in and take our time to find the property we wanted, but this wasn't an option for us. We had three dogs to bring with us (two of whom were St. Bernards) and it would have been virtually impossible to find somebody willing to let their property to us. Even if we had, I would have been constantly stressing about the inevitable mess the dogs would make. The St. Bernards were very young (only a year old) and were still quite prone to chewing, not to mention the slobber, hair and the mess from their huge paws. Also, it would be difficult to try and settle the children in school and then move them again when we found a house to buy.

So, we decided that we would have to try and tie in the sale in the UK with the purchase of a property in France and make the move in one go. The difficulty with this of course, is that the selling process in the UK is not at all cut and dried, as anyone who has endured the process is well aware. You can never really be sure if it's going to go ahead until you exchange contracts, which is often the week before moving (or even the day before sometimes). In France on the other hand they have a much fairer system. You usually sign a preliminary contract within a week of making the offer, then you have a seven day cooling off period after which time you pay a 10% deposit and if you don't go ahead with the sale, you lose your deposit. There are certain clauses you can put into the contract – i.e., if you can't get a mortgage you can withdraw without losing your deposit, etc., but at least with this system you make an actual commitment to buy very early on in the buying process. So many buyers in the UK make offers on properties without being fully committed, as they know they can pull out whenever they want. Also, in France, the whole process usually takes about three months and can be even quicker in some cases (unless it's over the month of August in which case you can add a month as nothing gets done in France in August). In the UK, it's very rare to have a sale go through in three months – in my experience, six months is more usual.

It was so exciting to finally be able to look at these properties and know we could make an offer with the confidence that we had a buyer for our own property. The first thing we did was look up the details of the property in Revel – but we couldn't find it. The property had either been sold or withdrawn from the market. It seemed significant to us that it had been there all this time, then, just when we were able to do something about it, it had gone. We were just entering a busy period for us at the guest house, as it was Easter and there was no way we could organise a trip together to go back to France. Someone had to stay and run the guest house. So, we arranged for Gary to return with Ryan to try and find us a home. We put together another list of properties and organised the viewings with the agents before leaving (as usual). Whilst Gary was in France, we heard from Frans that the big factory-like watermill in the Haute-Garonne had come back onto the market, as the buyers couldn't raise a mortgage. We jumped at the chance and Gary went to view it. I'd really studied the photos and the plan so thoroughly that I felt like I knew the property even though I hadn't seen it. He called me after the viewing:

"I really like it, it's an incredible building – the possibilities are endless. But as I was leaving there was another couple coming to look at it. What do you think we should do?"

"Make an offer" I said

"Are you sure? You haven't even seen it!"

"I know, but I really do feel like I know the property and we don't want to lose it now, so make the offer". Now, those who know me well would appreciate what a totally out of character thing this was for me to say. Gary is the reckless one, I'm the sensible, cautious one, but something inside told me it was the right thing to do. So that's what he did. He called me back after he'd put the offer in. Apparently, Frans had dismissed the offer and said he didn't think the owners would consider it. There was a lot of interest in the Mill, it had already sold once at a higher price (although this had fallen through). Gary stuck to the price though – it was as much as we could afford – anymore and we would have nothing left to do any of the renovations needed. After a nail-biting few hours, Frans got back to us to say the offer had been accepted– we couldn't believe it.

A week later we flew over together for one night to sign the *compromis de vente* (the preliminary contract). I viewed the property for the first time on the morning before signing the contract and I think Frans was worried I wouldn't like it, but on the contrary - I loved it. It was all that I thought it would be and more. As we drove down the lane leading up to the *Moulin*, I can still remember the excitement building within me. Nothing quite prepares you for the size of the building on first sight and it doesn't matter how often we tell people how big it is, everyone is overwhelmed when they see it. I think most people are frightened by the sheer size of it, but I found it exciting thinking about the endless possibilities. I loved the land, the lake, the woodland, the canal, the old *pigeonnièr* and the charming tumbledown outbuildings. It was early May and even though it was a dull day, it was a blaze of spring colour, wildflowers and blossoms everywhere. I couldn't quite believe that soon this could all be ours, when only ten years earlier we had been homeless and penniless with little hope for the future...

Inside the building was a maze of rooms – nothing was finished, but the plumbing was in place and the roof looked sound. The electrics were a bit of a nightmare with wires all over the place, so we knew we'd have some work to do there. However, we could live in it straight away and start renovating it gradually. The ground floor had not been renovated and looked like a factory still in parts, with large machinery, cogs and wheels hanging from the ceilings. The first floor had a very large (and very dated) kitchen and a large sitting/dining room – about 180 m^2 (about the size of the average four bed house in the UK). Then it had four partially renovated bedrooms on that floor (and three bathrooms). The second floor had a large unconverted area above the sitting room and then a further five bedrooms, partially renovated, with the pipe work there for bathrooms, but no bathrooms fitted. The third floor was an attic, but with windows and standing height, so potential additional living space and it covered about 200 m^2. In addition to this, there was a three-bedroom house on the end of the building in need of total renovation, but with the pipe work there already. We knew it was a massive project and it would probably be at least ten to fifteen years before we achieved everything we wanted to do, as we didn't have a large amount of money available to do all the renovations necessary. But the possibilities were as endless as the money we would need to carry them out, although we didn't let a little thing like that bother us! It wasn't just the house that attracted us though, we were also very happy with the situation of the property. It was rural without being isolated as it has two small towns within ten minutes' drive with all amenities; the larger town of Saint-Gaudens within twenty minutes and Toulouse was only one hour away with its international airport and direct links to many areas of the UK. Toulouse is the region's capital and is a very modern city - the fourth largest population in France. The property is also within two and a half hours' drive to either the Atlantic coast to the west or the Mediterranean coast to the east. To the south and about an hour's drive away is the border with Spain and an easy day trip. This part of Haute Garonne is very agricultural, and they don't grow grapes here commercially. Most of the crops are wheat and maize, and it's a beautiful patchwork of yellow sunflowers in July. It's only thirty minutes from the foothills of the Pyrenees and so all around the area you are never far from a breath-taking view of the mountains.

And so, on the 7th May 2004 we signed the *compromis de vente* and committed ourselves (and our children) to a new life. During the signing of the contract, our *notaire* (solicitor) noticed that it was our wedding anniversary (we were married on 7th May 1988). After the signing Frans asked:

"So, it's your wedding anniversary today - congratulations. What plans do you have for this evening?"

"Thanks, we thought we'd go to the *auberge* at the end of the road, near the *Moulin...*"

"Yes, that's okay, but it's not too special. You should celebrate. I know a lovely restaurant not far away; it serves excellent food".

Gary and I looked at each other - money was really tight. We couldn't afford to spend too much. "Is it expensive?" we asked tentatively

"Don't worry about it, I'll call them, and the meal is on me".

"No, no we couldn't"

Frans wouldn't hear our protestations. He was going to treat us and that was final.

It was a fantastic meal in a lovely setting - quite unlike any other dining experience we had encountered. We weren't sure what to choose, so we went for the "*menu gourmand*" - five elegantly presented courses with a different wine with each course. Our very attentive (and rather camp) waiter was one of the owners and he very kindly talked us through the menu. He quickly realised from our stumbling French that we were English and started to explain the courses in English. It was very amusing watching him describe the parts of the duck we were being introduced to "Zis course 'as zee meat lightly grilled, I don't know 'ow you say it in Engleesh, but it comes from 'ere", he said, gesturing to the liver/kidney area of his body.

'Hmmm' I thought, 'I'm not too keen on offal, but I'll give it a go'. Whatever it was, it was cooked to perfection and was mouth-wateringly good. We also had our first taste of *foie gras* and although now I know what it is, I don't approve of the methods of extracting it, I must admit it was absolutely delicious. It was a very special meal and a fitting end to a truly memorable day. We felt so lucky and we had a whole new life ahead of us...

The stresses of buying and selling

It's one thing making the decision to move to a new country, but the practicalities of making it happen are quite another. The first major hurdle was selling our property in the UK. After we got back from our first visit to Southwest France, we contacted several estate agents and put our guest house on the market. We discussed it with my parents who had retained part of the house and converted it into a flat. At first, they said they would like to come with us – I know my father had always dreamed of moving abroad, but it had never been quite the right time for them. However, after giving it much thought, my mother panicked and decided she wasn't ready at the time. I know she felt torn because my father was keen, but there was also my sister living nearby, who was on her own with her nine-year-old daughter and seven-year-old severely autistic son. I understood it wasn't an easy decision and it was all going too quickly for her. After all, they hadn't even visited the area of France we were thinking of moving to, and so she had no way of visualising what life might be like for them there. So, they decided not to come with us, and we had to go ahead and sell the guest house part of the building and my parents retained ownership of the ground-floor flat. It made the property more difficult to sell, but we were sure there would be a buyer out there somewhere, it would just take us a little longer to find them.

As we had anticipated, it took some time before we had a serious offer on the property. We had lots of interest and a couple of silly offers, but we weren't in a rush. We wanted to make sure we had found the right area to move to and there was no point in selling our property too cheaply or we wouldn't have enough money to buy what we wanted. Just over a year after putting our house on the market, we finally had a couple interested who were cash buyers, they made a sensible offer and we gladly accepted it.

After Gary had made the original offer on the watermill in France without me, the seller's *notaire* then drew up the *compromis de vente*, which is signed within a week or so. In France it is normal for the *notaire* of the seller to handle the whole sale for both parties. However, as we were English and not used to this, we hired an English lawyer practising in France to handle the sale for us. It made us feel safer to be able to discuss everything in English. She checked through all the paperwork for us, gave us a translation and explained the process.

After signing the *compromis de vente* on the watermill, we were on a high - we had just signed for the house of our dreams, in an idyllic setting in Southwest France. We then had to sort out how we were going to get the deposit - we didn't have any spare money or savings, so the only option we had was to borrow the money. We went to see our bank, explained that we had made an offer on a house in France, we had buyers for our property in England and we needed to borrow the deposit money which would be paid back on completion of the house (hopefully about three months) to which they agreed. A word of warning, despite explaining to the bank that we would be paying the loan off on completion of the house, they failed to point out that there would be a heavy penalty to pay the loan off before the end of the three year term (a costly mistake that ate into our dwindling money for renovations). So, the loan was granted, the deposit money was transferred to the *notaire* in France and within three months we would be on our way to our new life in France. But of course, nothing is ever that simple.

The sale of our property in the UK was proceeding very slowly. Our solicitor had received some queries from our buyer in the beginning, but after two months we still didn't seem to be any closer to exchanging contracts. Our provisional final signing date for the watermill for the end of July was drawing closer and closer and we were starting to get concerned. Then, at the beginning of July, our worse fears were realised - our buyer dropped out of the sale because they couldn't raise the bank loan they needed. They had told us initially that they were cash buyers, but it transpired that they were borrowing part of the money against another property and that was causing the problem. We felt as though our world had come to an end – how on earth were we going to get another buyer and complete within three weeks? Gary phoned Frans our agent in France to give him the bad news. He wasn't at all sure that the owner would agree to extend the completion date. After all, he was completely in his right to insist that we stick to it, in which case we would have to lose our deposit or try to get a bridging loan – which was not an avenue we wanted to go down. After a few hours, Frans phoned us back and said that the current owner of the watermill was prepared to extend the completion date for a couple more months, which was a great relief. But he warned that he couldn't extend it more than that. We knew if we didn't find another buyer within a few weeks we would lose the watermill and our deposit.

It was a tense time, but miraculously within a week, we had another very interested buyer and this time they really meant business. We could breathe again, and it looked as though things would work out okay after all. We went from one extreme to the other – from hardly any contact at all from our first buyers, to an almost daily stream of questions and queries from our second buyer. Their solicitor was very thorough and bombarded our solicitor with endless demands. Firstly, they wanted to buy the double garage belonging to my parents who had retained this as part of their property. Although they weren't keen to lose the garage, my parents knew how important this sale was to us and agreed to sell it to our buyers and a price was agreed. Then the buyers wanted them to sign an agreement to give them first option to buy their flat at the going rate if ever they decided to sell, to which they also agreed. Then their solicitor advised them to get my parents to sign a paper to guarantee they weren't going to go bankrupt. I suppose they were worried that if they went bankrupt the flat could be repossessed and they would lose control of what would happen to it – so my parents dutifully signed it.

Their solicitor really seemed to be trying to cover every possible eventuality. About a month into the selling process, it was discovered that we had a problem with the status of our property with the planning office. Before we had decided to buy the property from him, my father had been granted planning permission to convert the building into four flats in 2000. We then offered to buy the property from him and he retained one of the proposed flats on the ground floor, we occupied the top floor (which was already a flat) and we continued to run the rest of the building as a guest house. However, because the conversion of the flat had started, it apparently made the property's status of "guest house" no longer valid. The planning permission had been to convert the property into four flats, not into one flat and the rest of the building remaining as a guest house. Why this hadn't come up sooner than this I don't know, as it should have been highlighted when we bought the property.

We thought we had covered everything – my parents had a leasehold on the flat and the flat had been signed off as meeting building regulations by the Building Control only a few months before. We had to go to the planning office and explain the situation. Initially the person we saw was very sympathetic. He could foresee no problems with the application as the guest house had been running for 20 years and we should get confirmation of this within a week or so.

Two weeks later we received a phone call from a different planning officer who oversaw our application to say that he was coming out to view the flat before he could give his approval for the planning permission. A simple task it would seem. Well, the planning officer came to visit us and seemed pleasant enough – a very tall and slightly awkward guy who never seemed to be able to look you in the eye when you were talking to him (always a bit suspicious). We showed him the flat and the rest of the building.

Firstly, in the garden he noticed that the bedroom of the flat overlooked the back garden of the guest house – he mumbled something about lack of privacy for the flat owners. He suggested putting in a frosted glass window – which was not a problem for us to do (a bit annoying, but not impossible) and other than that all seemed OK. So, relieved, we left it at that and waited for news on our planning application.

Three weeks later and we had heard nothing, so I decided to phone the planning officer to find out how things were progressing. He told me that he was recommending that the planning permission be granted, but with a couple of conditions, one of which would be concerning the amenity space. When I pushed him to confirm exactly what he meant by this he was very evasive and said he would call me back later. When he did call me back, he told me the planning permission would be granted, but with a clause to say it was for the current ownership only – to be reassessed when the flat changed ownership. What use was that? Who on earth in their right mind would buy our guest house with planning permission that would become invalid if the flat was sold? It was crazy!

We decided to go down to the planning office together and thrash it out with him. The flat currently had a small courtyard at the side of the property sufficient to store bins, etc, but not a garden as such. My parents owned the flat and were not concerned about the lack of garden – they had no need or wish for a garden. The building was situated just off the sea front and so they had plenty of outside space when they wanted and no need for any upkeep. We met with the planning officer and explained that planning permission granted for present ownership only was not acceptable. He said the only way that we could get the planning permission granted would be to provide a portion of the back garden of the guest house to give the flat a garden to improve their 'quality of life'.

"How much garden?", Gary asked. After trying to evade the question, we pushed him into a corner and got him to commit, "About 10' x 6'" was his reply!

When we pressed him about the privacy, he'd said was so important – how would this improve their privacy? He said that this area would have to be fenced with a 6' high fence to provide privacy. It was at this point that Gary just saw red, he jumped out of his seat and said through gritted teeth:

"This is getting beyond a joke; don't you realise you are messing with our lives!"

I had to literally hold Gary back as he was the closest I have ever seen him to punching the guy in the face. Gary is usually very calm and laid back and on the rare instances where he loses his temper, he will walk away from the situation to calm himself down. But this was different – this man was causing so much unnecessary stress for us; he probably had no idea of how significant his petty mindedness was to our future. Or maybe he did and that's why he did it to make himself feel powerful. Whatever the reason, Gary punching him on the nose was not going to solve anything, so I pulled him away and we left the office.

So, the fact remained that in order to for planning permission to be granted, we had to force my parents to have a postage stamp sized garden they didn't want and then fence it with a high fence which would then block out the light to their bedroom. Does every flat in the country have a garden? On top of that and more importantly to our sale – our buyers were not at all happy with the thought of losing a chunk of the already small garden and having a large fence erected – they were on the brink of pulling out of the deal altogether. The stupid thing was that we all knew this was a pointless exercise as the chances were that my parents would sell the flat in a few years to the new owners and the house would be reunited under one ownership.

I really can't describe the amount of stress we were under at that time – we were at the end of our tether and so close to losing everything we'd worked so hard to gain. All because of a stupid planning officer who had nothing better to do with his time than find problems where there were none. I wrote faxes and letters outlining the details of the case and asked that it be considered during the planning meeting. My father-in-law, who couldn't believe the problems we were having, called them too and came to the planning office with me to hand over a statement I had written to be included in the planning meeting. It was a last-ditch attempt to appeal to their human side – we felt it was futile, but it was all we could do.

A week later and the date for our planning permission to be considered had arrived. We waited anxiously all morning, wondering what our fate would be – the anticipation was killing me. At the end of the morning Gary rang the planning office to see what the decision had been, and he was put through to the head planning officer.

"I'm sorry Mr McArthur but we had to make a few changes to the conditions recommended on the planning consent", Oh no! Not more, not now! I saw Gary's face drop and I looked at him anxiously waiting for him to tell me what was going on.

"Yes, Mr McArthur, we decided to remove the condition to include a garden." Gary couldn't quite believe what he had just heard.

"What do you mean?" He said puzzled.

"Well, we decided that we couldn't possibly stipulate what size the garden should be, so removed the condition altogether." he replied.

I could see the look of relief and joy all mixed together on Gary's face and he said,

"If you were here now right now, I'd give you a big kiss."

"A handshake would suffice Mr McArthur", was his dry reply. "I'll send it in the post", he continued,

"No, no, we're coming over to the planning office right now to get it", Gary replied. We couldn't quite believe it and wouldn't until we had the hard evidence in our hands. So, we sped off to the planning office to pick it up, feeling dazed at this development - it was quite surreal. Not in our wildest dreams had we thought that they'd actually remove the clauses altogether. But, sure enough, there it was in black and white - planning consent granted for the building to be a guest house with one separate residential flat and NO CLAUSES. It seems the head of planning had seen sense and our persistent phone calls and letters had made a difference after all. All those weeks of worry and stress caused by that one unhelpful planning officer - a lot of fuss about nothing! Our buyers were of course relieved that all had been agreed and they could keep the whole garden - so the sale was back on track.

Now all the obstacles had been removed, we could get on with the business of arranging the not inconsiderable logistics of coordinating a move of this size. In preparation, I had been reading and rereading all the books on living and working in France, starting a business in

France as well as many real life stories of living there – anything I thought would help me to prepare us both physically and mentally for the move. We had already started reducing our belongings – it wasn't worth hiring a big removals van to move us, as much of our furniture was being sold with the guest house and every penny counted. I spent a lot of time selling all our old records, games, books, etc. on eBay. I was amazed at the price we got for some of the items – especially a lot of Gary's old records like a scratched Jimmy Hendrix LP and classic album cover, Beatles LPs, etc. One of our biggest gains was for an expansion pack for a Board Game called Hero Quest. It was boxed and still in its cellophane – never opened. I'd bought it for Gary about ten years before and it had got packed into a box in a previous move and forgotten about – it probably cost about £10 at the time and it sold on eBay for over £100! We raised over £1000 selling things we didn't need or want.

The time was drawing nearer, and the finer details of the move were being planned – boxes were being packed and labelled, and we were getting the dogs pet passports and jabs sorted. What an expensive waste of time that was. Had we realised it wasn't necessary if you didn't intend to bring the dogs back to England, then we wouldn't have bothered. We spent loads of money on visits to the vets to make sure they had all their rabies jabs, etc., up to date and then we weren't even stopped or asked to show anything on the way.

One difficulty was how to coordinate the two moves to coincide. We couldn't sign for the watermill in France until the money was cleared with the *notaire* and this would take a few days. We were moving out of our house in England on a Friday which meant the money wouldn't be with the *notaire* until at least the middle of the following week. So, what were we going to do for those few days before we took ownership? It was complicated because we had the dogs and so wouldn't be able to stay in a B&B. We discussed the problem with our agent Frans and asked if the current owner would mind us camping on the land with the dogs until we could take ownership. Luckily the owner was very easy going and said he was happy for us to have the keys to the house and stay there for the few days before the contracts were signed. It was a big headache solved for us and we were very grateful to him for allowing us to do that.

I couldn't believe that things finally seemed to be going to plan – it was really going to happen; we were going to live in France. But there was one niggling suspicion that crept into my mind, something I hadn't planned for or even considered despite my hours of preparation, thinking ahead, writing lists and trying to cover all the possible scenarios. As if moving to a different country with three children and three dogs wasn't hard enough, two weeks before we were due to leave that niggling suspicion was confirmed when I discovered I was pregnant with our fourth child!

It was a shock; I really hadn't planned on that at all. Shortly after I'd found out I went next door to my mum's to pick up James as she had been looking after him for me as she often did (handy having parents living next door, I'd really miss that).

My mum looked up from her book and said, "That blouse looks lovely on you Nicks".

"Thanks Mum, but I don't think it will be fitting me for much longer".

She gave me a startled look "Oh no, you're not pregnant again are you!"

"Yes, Mum I am, and it will be fine, it always is", if I said it often enough, maybe it would be true...

We're going to Live in France!

A t last, on 30th September 2004, after eighteen months of planning, we finally set off at 6am in the morning from my sister's house in Westgate-on-Sea, to make the 1100km journey to our new home and new life in France. Gary and I travelled up front in our Bongo Friendee (a nine-seater people carrier) with James and Ryan behind. Matthew was staying at school as it was term time – it felt strange leaving without him and must have felt even stranger for him. The vehicle was filled to the brim with last minute bits and pieces and the three dogs (Amber and Ruby the one-year-old St. Bernards and Katie our eight-year-old black lab) sedated in the back. Behind us, our friend Mike and my sister Debbie were travelling in a hired seven-ton van carrying all our worldly goods. They were coming along for a few days to help us when we got there and then they were both going to drive back to England and return the van, and we were staying to start our new life.

Although we had visited France many times over the previous eighteen months or so, this was the first time we had travelled down by road as we normally took the plane. We'd planned our route, no satnav just good old-fashioned map books, had made our picnic and we were on our way!

First stop was Folkestone – we decided to go via the Eurotunnel and there we hit our first problem. We went through the check-in gates ahead of Mike and Debbie.

"Have you got any gas bottles on board", the official asked.

"No", Gary truthfully replied. However, this question made us both feel very uncomfortable. Gary had decided last minute, to pack a tiny camping gas bottle as an emergency when we arrived in France. We would be arriving late evening and Debbie, the children and I were going to stay in a B & B. Gary and Mike were going to camp outside our new house with the dogs. Gary thought the camping bottle might be handy to make a cup of tea or something when they arrived. We hadn't realised you weren't allowed to travel with gas bottles through the tunnel. It was packed in the van behind us. As we moved forward, Mike pulled up into the check in booth. Gary and I exchanged worried glances.

"I hope he doesn't say yes", Gary articulated what I was thinking.

"I know - do you know where you packed it?"

"Haven't a clue", he replied. Unfortunately, Mike owned up and told them he had a gas bottle on board. Of course, we hunted and hunted but couldn't find it and so they decided the van would have to be scanned. We were a little worried as at the last-minute Gary had also shoved in an old air rifle in case he needed it when we got there. It was a gun that had been given to us by a friend who found it in a skip (he'd never used it), but he thought it might come in handy. We were concerned that the scanner would pick this up and delay our journey even longer. All this took quite some time and so we missed our 7am crossing - we were getting very edgy - were we going to be stopped at the final hurdle! After the scan showed nothing (not even the gun), we were allowed to go through and caught the next crossing - what a relief!

It was our first time through the tunnel, we normally took the ferry but because we had the dogs it was more practical to go on the train as you stay in your car all the way, and it is of course much quicker than the ferry, except of course when you get held up and searched! At long last we were ready to take our place - it seemed strange driving onto a train, squeezed into the long carriages like sardines. The entire thirty minutes or so it takes to cross the channel is spent sitting in your vehicle, with nothing to look at apart from the posters on the walls. It was very tedious until, about halfway through the tunnel, I heard those all too familiar words that all parents fear! "Mummy, I feel sick"! Oh no, too late! James was sick all over himself and the car seat. I had to clamber into the back and clear it up as best I could, luckily, I had a change of clothes handy, but we had the sweet aroma of vomit all the way after that! Don't you just love long journeys with small children! And we hadn't even entered France yet!

On French soil at long last, the journey from Calais to Paris was fairly uneventful, the roads were reasonably clear, and we seemed to be making good headway. We stopped once at a service station to get some refreshments and stretch our legs. We opened the back to let the dogs out and they just looked at us, bleary eyed. Gary had to physically pull them out to give them a chance to stretch and relieve themselves. Luckily service areas in France are generally very good and cater well for travellers. The facilities for campers are particularly good with areas to top up with water, showers and often facilities for emptying your grey water too. They also have "aires" which are places to stop in between service stations that have picnic areas and often showers and toilets and are usually pleasantly placed. We found a free picnic table and got out our lunch. The French take their picnicking very seriously. There was a family on the bench near us who got out their picnic hamper which not only included a vast array of plastic containers filled with delicious looking food, but also tablecloth, flowers, glasses and wine. It made our plastic bag full of cheese and pickle rolls, a packet of crisps and a KitKat look rather pathetic. I could see I had a lot to learn!

Lunch was swiftly eaten and then we were on the road again. Once we hit Paris, things started to go a bit pear-shaped. The passage around Paris was not an easy one, there was no main ring road and the signs were very confusing. Whatever time you hit it doesn't seem to matter – it's always really busy. All the roads have several numbers, which often change for no apparent reason and we inevitably took a wrong turning. It was several kilometres before we realised we had gone wrong and we all pulled over to have a look at the maps and try to work out where we were. We were hot and bothered, and it was some time along that road before we had the opportunity to turn back the way we had come. It was quite a costly mistake to make and added a considerable amount of time to our journey. It has always made me wary of going around Paris and these days if I ever drive back to the UK I tend to go via Rouen, as it's much easier and often quicker. I also use a satnav, as I'm often driving alone (not that I do it very often) and would find it impossible to check the map and drive at the same time. Most of the journey is straightforward, there's just one section that's a bit tricky and can lead to a costly mistake, and we just happened to find it.

We finally got to the other side of Paris after about six hours on the road (which was at least a couple of hours longer than it should have been). After Paris though, the journey was quite straightforward – it was basically one very long road. The first half on this road was very boring – just endless flat and uninteresting countryside and finally after what seemed like an endless time, we saw a sign for Toulouse (our nearest major city). Yes, at last a sign for Toulouse, only afterwards we noticed it said 470km – which was very deflating, especially when we knew that our final destination was another 90km after Toulouse! I wish they used miles – 290 miles sounds so much better than 470 kms! About two thirds of the way through the journey, we hit Limoges and then the countryside really started to get interesting, unfortunately it was dark by the time we got this far, as we had to drive fairly slowly and stop several times for the children and the dogs. The fastest I've ever done the journey is in twelve hours door to door (but that was on my own), however, we didn't arrive at the guest house until midnight, after over eighteen hours of travelling. Although it wasn't the easiest of journeys, I was quite pleased at how well it had gone really. The children and the dogs were much better than I had anticipated. We were shattered though, and I took the children straight off to bed. It was so nice to snuggle down under the crisp white linen sheets. I was so tired I hardly remember my head hitting the pillow. While I was drifting into a deep sleep, Gary and Mike travelled the extra 20 minutes to camp outside our new house with the dogs.

The next morning, we woke to blazing sunshine. The B & B we were staying in was an old French manor house, with very comfortable classical rooms and a beautiful romantic style garden. Gary and I had stayed the night there when we had come to sign the *compromis de vente*. As we sat down for a continental breakfast of fresh croissants, homemade jam, cake and coffee, Gary walked through the dining room door with a look on his face that told me, something had happened.

"Notice anything?" he asked.

"What on earth has happened to you?" I noticed his clothes were damp. He sat awkwardly on the edge of a chair so he wouldn't get it wet and told us about his unfortunate night at the watermill, over breakfast.

It was nearly 1am before they had arrived at the property and they had parked the van up outside the front. Gary had let the dogs out for a stretch before bed. They were still a bit slow and bleary eyed from the journey and it was pitch black. Ruby (one of the St. Bernards) was very dopey – she is even when she hasn't been sedated. Unfortunately, she didn't realise there was a canal just in front of the car (having never been there before). She stumbled out of the back of the car and before Gary could stop her, she ran straight into the canal and then couldn't get out. Gary had had to pull her out and got soaking wet in the process. I had the suitcase with a change of clothes for us all with me in the nice dry and warm B & B and so Gary had had to try and sleep in the van in his wet clothes – not the best start to our new adventure, but he was so tired he had managed to get a little broken sleep.

After breakfast, Gary went up to our room showered and changed. Despite the previous night's mishap, he was raring to go. It was so exciting to think we were here at last and about to start our new life. We were keen to get to the *Moulin* and start unpacking and settling in. There was so much to do and explore we couldn't wait!

What have we got Toulouse?

PART 2

Life in France - The early years

What have we got Toulouse?

Snakes, bats and rats!

We pulled up outside our new home at about 10am with van, people carrier, kids, dogs and all our worldly possessions. God knows what our new neighbours thought! They warily handed over the key the current owner had entrusted to them. We introduced ourselves and tried to have a friendly chat. It wasn't easy as our French was limited and their English was non-existent! Debbie spoke the most French, but she didn't have any more success. We were trying to find out where we could get some bread. We asked in our best French about where to get "du pain" and they looked at us blankly. Lots of shrugging, scratching heads and narrowing of eyes followed. We tried again, no joy. Then we tried miming and eventually we managed to communicate our need for sustenance:

"Ah, du peng" they cried! This was our first encounter with the unusual accent the locals have here. Many words finish with an "eng" sound – "de**meng**" (for "demain"), "se**meng**" (for "semaine"), "proch**eng**" (for "prochaine"). Our neighbours informed us that a bread van came every Monday and Thursday, but as it was a Saturday we were out of luck, we would have to make a trip to the local supermarket.

First however, we needed to explore, so armed with the key we pushed open the door to this enormous beast of a building, which we were now to call home. It was much dustier and dirtier than I had remembered. In the entrance hall there were piles of old, rotting wood stacked up, everything was covered in a thick layer of dust and huge cobwebs hung from the ceilings. It was like stepping into Sleeping Beauty's castle after she'd been asleep for 100 years.

The *Moulin* had been the former owner's second home and he had never really lived in it properly for the five years he had owned it. We had been told that he had mainly used it for parties – and some very good parties they must have been too, judging from the amount of confetti, party hats and bottles we discovered around the house. I don't think he had been in the house since we had signed the *compromis de vente* six months earlier, as the house and grounds lay untouched. On further exploring our new home, we soon discovered that a number of unwanted guests had taken up residence.

As we walked up the stairs there were some strange dark brown sticky stains on the marbled steps. What on earth was that I wondered? We looked up and discovered the culprits - a couple of bats were hanging from the ceiling beams. Then we ventured into the main living area on the first floor. Debbie was impressed by the size of the sitting room. She loved it and understood what we saw in it, but I think she (like most people) thought we were more than slightly mad to take on such a huge project. As we wandered through the rooms, we found more and more evidence of bats and lots of rat droppings. We knew they were rats and not mice by the large size of the droppings. We'd lived in the country before and have had mice lots of times, but never rats and bats!

"Nikki, keep James and the dogs away!" I heard Gary shout from the hall below. He had started moving the logs at the entrance only to discover a large and dangerous looking snake. On further investigation, he found several more, which we later discovered were in fact the venomous asp viper. We kept away whilst he cleared out all the wood carefully and moved all the snakes a safe distance away from the house. It was several years before they stopped coming back into the house. We still occasionally find large snake skins lying in the road outside the front door.

Some doubts were starting to creep in. What on earth had we let ourselves in for! But these doubts didn't last long, there was so much to do, no time for second thoughts. Once the entrance was clear, Debbie and I drove off with two-year-old James in search of a supermarket to find some food and cleaning products. We took the road into our nearest town and we were stunned that we could see the Pyrenees in all their splendour. It had been cloudy when I visited the house before and so I had no idea how close the mountains were and how breath-taking the view was.

"You're so lucky to be living here – I wish it was me!", Debbie sighed. Yes, we were very fortunate, but luck didn't really have anything to do with it. Hard work and single-minded determination had got us here - and perhaps a little madness.

We arrived at the supermarket and as James had fallen asleep, Debbie stayed in the car with him. I went into the shop alone and started wandering around the aisles trying to find all the things we needed. It always takes longer shopping in a new supermarket, but when that supermarket is in another country and everything is in a different language, it takes even longer. I heard some announcements being made over the loudspeaker but didn't pay attention and carried on. After a few moments Debbie came rushing in – "Nicks hurry up, they're closing!" I hadn't realised that the whole shop was closing around me – the shutters were half pulled down, they were closing for lunch. Closing for lunch? It takes some getting used to when you come from England with 24hour shopping. I hadn't realised how much I had taken 'open all hours' for granted before I moved here. As well as closing between 12-2pm, most shops close by 7pm and NOTHING is open on a Sunday! (Also, the petrol stations sell fuel and that's all! No tobacco, no alcohol, no shop, just petrol, diesel and gas bottles!) I rushed to the checkout, paid for my purchases and we went home. Home – I live in France! I couldn't quite believe that after all that planning and stress, I was actually living in France. That would take some getting used to!

After a quick lunch of French bread, cheese and pâté, we got started on the kitchen which took some time to clean. It was huge with a vast amount of very dated seventies style cupboards with teak-coloured melamine doors. It wasn't what I wanted, but it was functional. There was a fitted gas hob, which again was dated but worked, an electric tabletop oven which had seen better days and that was it. A door opening out onto a balcony, which unfortunately was without railings. This was going to be one of the first things Gary would have to try and make safe, so that James didn't go tumbling down. The greatest evidence of rats was in the kitchen – all the work surfaces and the top of the kitchen wall cupboards were thick with droppings, grease and dust – yuck! We put our gloves on and got scrubbing! It took most of the day to get it clean, but I felt much better when it was done. While Debbie and I were cleaning, Gary and Mike were emptying the van of all our belongings. We hadn't brought much – two sofas, one double and bunk beds, a cot, boxes of kitchen utensils, books, toys, personal items and clothing. Our two sofas looked completely lost in our new 90 m^2 sitting room! The owners had left a few items of furniture – a big old kitchen table and some rickety chairs, which we put to good use (and actually continued using for the next six years until our new kitchen was built!).

That evening we sat on the sofas in our huge empty sitting room, drinking wine, while a couple of bats swooped around the room. It wasn't really frightening, just a bit surreal. We didn't need to do anything to get rid of the bats – once they realised we were here to stay, they disappeared from inside the house, but we do still find them roosting in the shutters outside. We had to put poison down for the rats unfortunately, but we were careful to put it in places the dogs and kids couldn't get to and eventually they disappeared.

The next day we said our goodbyes to Debbie and Mike who set off with the van back to England. It was sad to see them go, but we had so much to get on with, we had no time to dwell on it. Onwards and upwards!

It's surprising what you take for granted and it's not until you move to another country that you realise it. France is not so far from the UK, but almost everything you try to buy is totally different. Basic food stuffs like flour for instance – I was surprised it wasn't the same as in the UK. Self-raising flour isn't available, their equivalent is *farine à gâteaux*, but it doesn't have any raising agent, so sponge cakes won't rise without adding baking soda. Fresh milk was not so common in supermarkets at that time, most people used UHT milk. It took us a while to get used to it, but it's much more practical. It doesn't bother me anymore, but many UK visitors miss fresh milk. It was hard to find cheddar and I know France has a multitude of delicious cheeses, but there's nothing to replace cheddar for cheese on toast! You'll be hard pushed to find bacon (in the same way that we are used to in the UK); there are rarely baked beans, just haricots beans in tomato sauce which isn't even close. There is also not such a wide choice of crisps, snacks, biscuits and spices are limited too. The French aren't as keen on spicy food as the Brits, so if you like a curry, stock up on some curry pastes and spices before you come.

We couldn't find Branston Pickle or any type of pickle, peanut butter, salad cream and Marmite. French tea is not great as it is very weak compared to the British taste. Most Brits stock up on teabags if nothing else when they go back to the UK to visit. All the French who have tried our tea prefer it too.

Paint is a product many Brits source from the UK - it's much more expensive in France (often more than double the price) and thinner than the UK equivalent. Second-hand goods (cars, furniture, etc.) are often more expensive too. Pillowcases - I could only find square ones and all my pillows were rectangles! These are just a few examples of the everyday differences that seem very strange and not at all what I expected to find on moving here.

One of the biggest problems we had in the beginning was finding the best places to buy the appliances we needed. We had to buy all our white goods (washing machine, tumble dryer, fridge, freezer, etc.). We thought it a good idea to start off in a major town and our closest was Saint-Gaudens. First, we took a look in an electrical shop in the centre and couldn't believe the prices (significantly more than we were used to paying in the UK). I felt totally lost - in England we knew exactly where to go to get what we wanted, even if we moved to a different part of the country, we could still find a Curry's or an Argos, but here everything was different. We didn't really know anyone either, so it was difficult to find someone to ask for advice. After a couple of failed attempts, we spoke to Frans our estate agent and he recommended a shop in our small local town, which was only ten minutes away. After driving around for a while (and it's not a very big town), we found the shop. From the outside you couldn't really see what they sold, but inside it was quite a big store with a large range of white goods, furniture, kitchen and bathroom fittings, ranging from fairly reasonable to very expensive. We managed to kit our kitchen out for a reasonable cost.

At this stage we had a fridge to store our food, we had a washing machine and tumble dryer to look after the washing and drying of our clothes, now all we needed was some furniture to fill up the vast empty rooms and start making this factory sized property into a home. We didn't have enough money for antiques and to be honest even if we did, we wouldn't buy any because either the dogs or kids would ruin them. We didn't want to go for too modern a style as it wouldn't have looked right in the house, so we needed to find a second-hand shop with some reasonably priced furniture. First, we followed some signs to a local *brocante* to see what they had to offer. A *brocante* can either be a second-hand market (like a flea market or boot fair in the UK) or a permanent shop selling second hand/antique items, mainly furniture. This particular *brocante* was a permanent fixture in a large old barn, on the edge of a local village. They had some lovely items in excellent condition and some more "ripe for refurbishment". We bought a couple of tables and units to stand in our hall, but we couldn't afford to furnish the whole house there. We have since found that *vide-greniers* are sometimes very good places to pick up second-hand bargains. *Vide-grenier* means literally "empty hayloft", presumably as most people store a lot of their unwanted items in the hayloft or attic. It is the closest thing you get here to the boot fairs, which are so popular in the UK. Most towns and larger villages hold a *vide-grenier* once or twice a year where mainly local people clear out their old stuff, with the occasional antique trader at some of the larger ones. I often find that the items on sale at a *vide-grenier* and second-hand shops are a lot more expensive than you would expect in the UK. There are several internet sites you can use to buy second-hand items www.leboncoin.fr, www.vivastreet.fr, www.paruvendu.fr. English speaking groups on Facebook are another good place to pick up a bargain, but they weren't around when we moved here. There's also French Ebay, but we've found that this is not as popular as it is in England and so you don't have a good choice of items.

71

A family moving to France

Someone recommended we pay a visit to Emmaus, a second-hand shop found in the bigger town of Saint-Gaudens. There we managed to find lots of very reasonably priced second-hand furniture and they would deliver for a small charge, which was even better. Emmaus is a charitable organisation, with "communities" all over France and other parts of the world. It was founded by Abbé Pierre, a very famous Catholic priest and former member of the French Resistance. The "Communities" provide shelter, work and support for the homeless and needy, who work in the second-hand centres selling, delivering and collecting the furniture, clothes and *bric à brac*. The items they sell are provided by donations and the proceeds go to help the needy. It's a very good idea and works extremely well. Another good place to find second-hand furniture, is at a "troc" or "*dépot vente*". These are second-hand shops where you can take your furniture or other items to be sold and they sell it for you and take a commission when it is sold.

Quite high up on our list of priorities was to get our telephone installed. A simple enough task you would think, but not in France! Because of our poor command of French at the time, Frans came with us to France Telecom in Saint-Gaudens. We were primed to take along our birth certificates and "*attestation de vente*" (a paper proving that we were the owners of the property). They asked a lot of questions about our needs and because we were planning on running a business and needed a fast internet package, they recommended that we go with a system called "Numeris", because it offered a faster speed dial up internet (there was no broadband in the area at the time). It seemed a good solution and we agreed. What we hadn't realised was, it would be three months before we had a telephone line. Every time we rang, they would tell us it would be next week, they had to upgrade the lines, etc. It was extremely frustrating, as we had so much to sort out and all we had to communicate with was our English mobile phone, which was costing us a fortune. We didn't realise until we got a bill for over £150 after the first month, that it was costing us when other people phoned us too. It was our first encounter with the poor customer service and absence of urgency here in France, something that I think we will never get fully used to. 'The customer is always wrong', seems to be the motto here, 'we don't care, that's just the way it is' seems to be another. One of the prices you pay for living in rural France and something you just have to learn to deal with. It was very difficult managing without a phone or internet connection for three months, but we are not alone. I've heard many other Brits complain about the length of time it took for their phone and internet connection to be installed and problems getting lines fixed when they inevitably go down.

I'm not going to go into the paperwork nitty-gritty here as so many "Living in France" guides cover that. What I will say though is that for some people it seems to be straightforward and for others it isn't. There doesn't seem to be any particular reason why, it just depends on which department you are in, your personal circumstances (and we all seem to be different), which *fonctionnaire* (civil servant) you see on the day and whether they are in a good mood or not. As EU residents (at the time) we didn't need a *carte de séjour* (residency permit), however Brexit (at the time of writing) has changed all this. As an EU resident you didn't need to change your UK driving licence (until it expires), but some gendarmes would say that you did – however, that again has changed due to Brexit causing thousands of Brits to try and exchange their licences before the deadline.

I can't say those early days were easy as they weren't. There was so much to sort out - the house needed a lot of work, the grounds needed developing, the children needed settling into schools, etc. For the first eighteen months Gary continued to work as a part-time lecturer in the UK. He would fly to England for a week and then be home and working on the house for two weeks. I had to cope on my own much of the time with the children, pregnancy, and then a new baby. We knew virtually no one and had no social life, but despite it all I was happy. I felt contented and so relieved to finally be here. I had mentally prepared myself that I would feel homesick at some point, but I'm still waiting for that!

First days of school

One of the first things I had to sort out was schools for Ryan and James. I had wanted them to go the *maternelle* and *Primaire* (infants and primary school) in local town of Boulogne-sur-Gesse, but when we arrived, I discovered we had to get *certificat d'inscription* (permission to start school) from our local *Mairie* in Escanecrabe. The *Maire* said they had to go to the local school and not wanting to upset anyone so soon, that's where they went. Ryan went to the local village school at Saman with a grand total of seventeen pupils aged eight to eleven and James to Ciadoux which had about forty pupils aged two to eight. James aged two and a half at the time didn't need to go to school of course, but we thought that going to school part time would be essential for him to learn the language. It would also give me a break as I was pregnant and on my own a lot, and James was a handful at the best of times.

Ryan's school was in a small village about 8km from us. It had one teacher for the seventeen pupils (including Ryan). I remember his first day as if it were yesterday. Up until then, I had been so busy finding a house, organising the move, settling in, etc., I hadn't had time to think about what it really meant for Ryan. Of course, we had consulted him all the way through about the move and he was happy and excited about it, but the reality of actually starting in a new school, when you hardly speak the language, is very different. He was so mature I often forgot he was only ten years old.

On the drive to the school on that first morning, I recall having a sudden dawning of the enormity of what we had just done in moving to France and the massive effect on our children. I parked the car outside the small village school, so different to the smart, large modern school he was used to in the UK. The look of bewilderment and panic on his face as we approached the building will live with me forever. He was being so brave, but I could see the tears welling up in his eyes. I dared not speak to him as I knew we'd both break down. I was so overcome with emotion, I felt like a volcano about to erupt. Luckily,

I managed to control myself long enough to speak with the teacher. We exchanged a few words, I gave him a kiss and a hug and left him at the top of the steps looking down, wide-eyed at the other children in the playground. He looked so alone and vulnerable, I felt like the worst mother in the world.

I cried all the way home and most of the day, 'What have we done? What have we done?' I kept repeating to myself. I felt so guilty that in all this time I hadn't truly appreciated what an enormous change we were enforcing on our children and of all of them, perhaps, the biggest change was for Ryan. He'd had six years of schooling in the UK and so could read and write well. He wasn't an overly confident child, but he made new friends easily and was very likable. He was popular with his teachers, as he was very willing, always ready to help others and was polite and well behaved. We had obviously weighed this all up before making the move and had considered that he would be able to manage the change well. But it doesn't matter how well you plan ahead; you never really know what it's going to be like until you do it. I couldn't help suddenly having enormous doubts on whether he was strong enough to cope.

I thought about him all day, I couldn't wait to pick him up and see how he'd got on. I was so relieved when he came ambling out of the classroom with a beaming smile on his face. He talked all the way home about how nice his teacher was, how difficult it was to understand what was going on, but that the teacher was very understanding, and the children all seemed very friendly. Apparently, he spent all of the playtime on that first day stood at the top of the steps looking on. The children tried to encourage him to play with them, but he was too scared to move. The following day he ventured from the step and never looked back. I'm not saying it was easy for him – it wasn't, but neither was there a single day when he didn't want to go to school and gradually it got easier and easier. He was lucky that he had a fantastic teacher, who was really sympathetic to his situation and spent a lot of time helping him. Also, the other children were very accepting of him and soon he settled into his new life and really enjoyed it.

We were lucky that Ryan's first experiences of school were so positive, however James, despite being younger, did not have a favourable start. We registered him at the local village school as we felt it would be good for him to mix with children of his own age and have some early exposure to the language. He had enjoyed going to a crèche a couple of times a week in England, so we thought he'd be fine. The *maternelle* schools here take children from two and a half (or when they are dry) until they're six years old. They are not compulsory, but most children go as it's free, the only charge being for the lunch if they stay. It's a really good start for the children.

James was still not dry when we arrived, so I spent the next couple of months (in between everything else), trying to get him "clean". It wasn't easy because he was so stubborn, but one day he just decided he was ready to do it and that was that. Within two days he was dry and out of nappies – hurrah! Shortly after Christmas when he was two and three quarters, he started at the local *maternelle* just a couple of mornings a week. The baby was due to be born in May and we felt it was best he started before he or she was born, as we didn't want him to feel he was being pushed out.

The school had about forty pupils split into two classes. In James's class, the ages ranged from two and a half to six years old. He was very keen to go in the beginning, but his enthusiasm quickly faded, and he would cling to me and cry when I left him. I ignored this at first as his older brothers had been just the same when they started playgroup and school in England. It's quite normal for young children to fear separation from their parents when they first start nursery, so I thought it was probably just a passing phase and understandable in the circumstances.

Whenever we picked him up from school, he seemed a bit subdued and often not his normal self. We thought it was probably just teething problems and he'd get used to it after a while. However, we started to have concerns about how he was being handled in school. Whenever we came a bit early to collect him, he was always on his own. It was really quite painful to see this, and we were very worried about how the whole school experience was affecting him.

We spoke to the teacher to see what she thought, she didn't seem to think there was a problem. We asked how she handled the language difficulties and she said that the *Directrice* (the head teacher) had told her not to speak any English to him at all or he'd never learn French. We told her that we thought it would be more useful if she spoke in French first and then used English if he didn't understand – after all he was only little. She refused. We were starting to get the impression that they just looked on James as an inconvenience. The teacher was very young and inexperienced and seemed more interested in devoting her time to the older children.

Several months passed and things weren't improving. James seemed to be withdrawing into himself more and more. The final straw came a few weeks before the baby was due. When we picked him up from school one day, he looked very disturbed. We could tell that there was something seriously up with him. He was silent and wide-eyed, like a rabbit caught in a car's headlights. It was as though he'd just witnessed something terrible. It transpired that the whole school had gone swimming that morning. He had been ill the previous day, so we didn't get the note about the swimming trip. James went off in the coach with all the other children. He probably didn't have a clue where he was going, as he didn't understand what was being said to him. When they arrived at the pool, all the other children got changed into their swimming costumes. All that is except James. He was made to sit on his own at the side of the pool and watch while all the other children splashed and played in the water. We know this because Ryan was on the other side of the pool at the time, as his school had a trip there too. He said it was heart breaking to witness. The worst of it was that he saw one of the helpers go and roll up his trousers because they were getting wet. He could see James' face light up thinking they were going to let him in the pool to paddle, only to be told off again and made to sit down like a naughty boy. Ryan said it was horrible and he felt like running over and cuddling him but had to stay with his group. When we heard this, we were sickened. Why didn't they phone us and ask for his swimming kit? Why didn't they just let him go in his pants – would it really have hurt? They don't normally bother about things like that here, I'm sure they could have got a spare towel or some spare trunks. Why didn't they realise how distressing this was to a three-year-old who didn't understand what was going on and why everyone else was having fun except him. It seemed obvious to us that this would only serve to compound the feelings of alienation he was having due to being English. Why couldn't they see that too? Did we really want people who were so insensitive and unfeeling to be responsible for our child? We decided that this was too much and we didn't care who we upset, our son was not going to this school and being subjected to this type of treatment ever again.

Gary went to the school the next day to see the teacher. I didn't know how he was going to communicate his feelings because his French was limited at the time, but I was heavily pregnant and too emotional to deal with it. When he arrived at the school and started to explain he wanted to speak to the teacher, one of the mums offered to translate for him. She was American but had a French husband and so spoke perfect French. Gary said he'd be okay, but she insisted (I think she probably regretted that later). He's not one to mince his words and this poor woman had to translate just how angry and disgusted he was with their treatment of our son. I'm sure he took the teacher down a peg or two and told her exactly what he thought of her. Whether they ever realised how wrong it was or not, we'll never know, but hopefully they'd think twice if the same situation ever arose again. We got the *certificat de radiation* (a form necessary for leaving a school) and never went back again.

We left it about a month, as it was so close to the birth of the baby, we didn't want to put James through any more trauma. A few weeks after the baby was born, we went to the *maternelle* in the local town. The *Directrice* there was a lovely lady and was very sympathetic. It's a bigger school and at the time had three classes of about fifteen pupils in each- one for *les petits* (two and a half to three year olds), one for *les moyens* (four to five year olds) and one for *les grands* (five to six year olds). We had to get another *certificat de scolarité* from our village *Mairie*. The *Maire* wasn't that happy about it and said we wouldn't be entitled to the free bus if he went to the town school. We explained that the village school didn't suit him, and we didn't care if he didn't get the bus, we had to do what was right for him. He reluctantly gave us the necessary *certificat de scolarité* and we took it to the town *Mairie* to show we had permission to transfer our son and then we were able to go to the school and inscribe him to start in the September. The difference was incredible – the teacher was very kind and spoke some English and he was with children of his own age. Very quickly he made friends and was a happier boy and we were happier parents.

James went from strength to strength and the teachers loved him – he was very good and very bright and was never knowingly naughty, so different to how he had been at the beginning. His teachers had nothing but praise for him and we were so glad that his bad experience at the first school didn't seem to have permanently damaged him. He now thankfully has no recollection of his first school.

The first year or so was tough all round. I knew it would be and had mentally prepared myself for it. Not only did we have to settle Ryan and James into school, but we also had to cope with Matthew not being around so much. We missed him terribly, but he coped very well with the arrangement. He often stayed at my parents or his local friends at the weekends. He was very mature for his age and so we gave him a lot of freedom within certain limits. He flew home by himself every holiday as he was allowed to do this from age fourteen on. It was always a little difficult when he first came home as the family dynamics would change from Ryan being the eldest to Matthew again, but he'd soon settle in. The most difficult time used to be the last few days of the holiday when he had to return to England as his mood would change. Whilst he enjoyed his school life, it was always tough to leave home and I think he was torn between two worlds. However, we all have no regrets and it was the best for him under the circumstances.

Building the dream

I remember Frans our estate agent's wise words when we first moved in, "Don't make any firm plans on major renovations, as you have to live in a house for a while before you can truly know what's going to work for you" and I couldn't agree more. Our plans for the building and life have changed enormously over time. I would always recommend spending some time living in any house that needs renovating and allow yourselves the opportunity to get a real feel for the building before embarking on any major work.

When we first moved here, Gary's work as a freelance horticultural lecturer in the UK financed our day to day living whilst we converted our first two *gîtes*. Our intention was that once we started letting the *gîtes*, the income would be enough for us to live on and Gary could stop commuting to England. We planned to get a third *gîte* (a two-bed apartment) up and running for the second year at which time we would start running residential gardening courses, operating in the low season (April, May, June and September, October). We were also aiming to be as self-sufficient as possible with growing our own vegetables and having a few animals (chickens, ducks, goats, sheep and pigs).

We had taken on such an enormous task, the only way we could cope with it was by breaking it into smaller projects and dealing with them one at a time. Yes, it was a huge building – all 1200 square metres of it and not many people in their right minds would have taken it on. But there were large parts of it we could just close the door on and forget about, and that is exactly what we did.

We hadn't got much money for renovations, so we planned to carry them out ourselves. There wasn't any major building work to do, just lots and lots of plaster-boarding, tiling, painting, and putting in several kitchens and bathrooms. We could manage that no problem!

Parts of the building are at least two hundred years old – maybe older and it was originally much smaller and constructed from limestone blocks. This was then built onto over the years. Some sections are built of stone and the most recent addition of the second and third floors to the middle section of the building, was carried out in the fifties/sixties. This could clearly be seen by the type of bricks used to build it and our neighbour Emile could remember this being done. There are three parts to the building which we have allocated three distinct functions. The right-hand side is the area we decided to make our home. It spreads over three floors - the ground floor had not been renovated and comprised of three rooms each approximately 60m^2 in size - all very dark and full of old bits of iron, rubbish, thick cobwebs and dust.

The first floor was the main living area, which covered about 180m^2 in total. As I said before, the sitting room was a massive 90m^2, its sheer size was very impressive, but it needed brightening up. The floor was tiled with terracotta tiles in a herringbone style, which gave the room a rather drab feel. There was a lovely original fireplace at the far end of the room, but other than that the room was featureless except for some large bars and wheels hanging from the ceiling at one end. We decided to keep these as a reminder of its industrial past as a working flourmill. The walls were painted a dirty mustard colour and the ceiling comprised of dark stained beams with the floorboards above exposed, with black industrial sized iron girders supporting them, running across the entire width of the room.

There was a large trapdoor measuring about 3m x 2m in the floor, which opened to the "cave" below and had a smaller trapdoor in the ceiling above which opened out to a pulley in the ceiling above that. Apparently, the lorries used to drive into the ground floor section of this part of the building and the flour sacks were hoisted using the pulley and lowered down onto the backs of the trucks to be taken away. This trapdoor was much later to become the opening down to our new kitchen (the old 'cave') which was accessed via a spiral staircase we had bought second hand from the Freeads in England shortly after moving here. It had sat in bits gathering dust and dog hair outside our bedroom door for over six years until we were finally ready to use it.

The sitting room then opened onto another room (about 45m^2) which had a large old table left in it, so I suppose it had been used as a dining area. We decided to separate this and make it our bedroom and an en-suite bathroom which we did in the first year of renovations. On one side of this room were double doors that led onto a balcony and on the other side an opening into the kitchen which was also about 45m^2. The large kitchen was fitted with wall and ceiling cupboards on two sides – more cupboards than I have ever had and thought I could ever fill. But I was wrong – I have found that no matter how many kitchen cupboards you have, you can always fill them! The cupboards were extremely dated and in imitation teak melamine with a white melamine work surface. However, despite their aged look, they were surprisingly well built and definitely usable. The walls were partially tiled around the inbuilt functional but dated gas hob with some old dark green tiles. There were two double sinks (which proved very handy) and were the old-fashioned ceramic type. This area had just bare chipboard walls – ready for tiling, but never completed. We even found boxes of tiles (the original packaging disintegrating with age) obviously intended for this area, but never used. The ceiling on this side of the building was sloped so that on one side of the kitchen, the ceiling was unusually high (about 6m) with the other side unusually low sloping down to around 1.5m where the sinks were. This meant that anyone over the height of 5' 5" would have to stoop to do the washing up - which is everyone in the family except the young children and my mum! In contrast, at the opposite end of the kitchen its height made it difficult to access without a scaffold tower to clean it and so it had twenty years of dust and cobwebs hanging down. This room was painted the same drab mustard colour and was very tired looking.

On one of the sides of the kitchen was a really old, but functional tabletop electric oven. To begin with, I used this and the gas hob for my cooking. I even attempted to cook our first Christmas dinner in it. We decided to have a goose, which we bought fresh from the local market at Samatan. It was huge and I struggled to squeeze it into the oven. I had never cooked goose before and hadn't realised just how much fat it produced. To my horror, I soon discovered this when it caught fire and smoke and flames were billowing out from the oven. After that, we had to keep emptying out the fat every so often and when it was finally cooked it was delicious, however, we ate our Christmas lunch at about 4pm that year.

One of my biggest disappointments with the house was that the kitchen was on the first floor. Part of my dream of living in France was the possibility of eating outdoors, but with the kitchen being on the first floor, there was no easy access to the outside. I really wanted a kitchen on the ground floor, but little did I know I would have to wait six years before this dream became a reality, but what a difference it made when it did! Also, those horrible dated kitchen cupboards were reused in our new kitchen as the carcasses were still very sound and my father in law, who was living nearby at the time, very kindly made new pine doors for them. They looked fantastic and the functioning of the kitchen worked so perfectly – just as I had visualised and dreamed it would. I can't describe how satisfying it is to plan something for so many years and then to see it all come to fruition – it gives me hope for the rest of the building. "Everything comes to she who waits!" has become my mantra. Once we had our new kitchen on the ground floor, the original kitchen was earmarked to become another bedroom and a family bathroom on one side leaving a large hallway leading to the balcony which would be lined with shelves and house our books. I had visions of taking a book onto the balcony to read in the sun, while the children played happily in the garden below (in my dreams). Actually, it was a further eight years before the family bathroom became a reality - but it was worth the wait. The rest of the old kitchen space I am now turning into my studio for writing, studying, drying herbs, following my creative hobbies such as painting and calligraphy, and for yoga and may eventually be a space for running workshops.

From the old kitchen on the first floor (soon to become my studio) is a wooden staircase that leads up to the second floor. You have to bend down to enter this area, as the ceiling is low, and it then opens out into what was just a large empty attic space full of junk and water tanks. It measured about 90m^2 and although the roof was sloped, there was enough head room here to convert this area into bedrooms. We put in more skylights and made this into a large playroom and three bedrooms for the children.

The middle section of the mill was converted into our holiday rental accommodation. The ground floor was again not renovated. There were two main entrance rooms and then to the left of the entrance hall was the area we call "the *Moulin*", which was (and still is) full of cogs and wheels hanging from the ceiling and houses a large heat exchange system. This was what we planned to use to generate our heating, but it turned out to be very inefficient. There are also lots of large complicated looking electrical panels which formed part of the system when the *Moulin* was generating electricity. The building was sold to us with two turbines. We were told one was functioning and the other needed some work to fix it. We have since found out that they are both so old fashioned it would probably be more practical to have a new system installed. It has always been our intention to do that someday, but that's one (of many things) we have planned for a later date when we have the money, time and energy to devote to it. This area is currently much the same as it was when we moved in except now it's full of our junk and for several years was overflowing with boxes of clothes and medical equipment destined for Syria (but that's another story). Our current plan for this room is to convert it into a Yoga/Meditation/lecture room for the courses and workshops we plan to run.

On the first floor of this middle section of the building, there was a long corridor with doors off to four partially renovated bedrooms with en-suite bathrooms. These were mainly clad in pine – so much so that we think the previous owner must have had a job lot. It was largely okay and so we decided to live with it for the time being, as there was so much else to do. One of our first jobs was to convert these four rooms into two one-bedroom self-contained apartments and to have them ready for letting by the following summer. This involved tiling two bathrooms, tiling 250m^2 of floor, plaster-boarding ceilings and walls, and fitting two kitchens and painting, lots and lots of painting.

The second floor had potentially five en-suite bedrooms, but none of the bathrooms were fitted, although the pipe work was in place. We had originally planned to make these into a further two apartments, but in the end, we settled on making one two-bedroom apartment which was completed in our second year. The other two rooms can be accessed from our living quarters and are used as a supplementary bedroom and en-suite bathroom for visitors and as a storage room.

The third floor runs across the entire length of the middle section of the building and covers about 250m² of usable loft space, as it has windows along the entire length and has reasonable head room. It could be an enormous meditation room, artist's studio, a penthouse suite, a games room (big enough to play football in in fact) and you can actually see the roof tiles, which is useful as the freak hail storms often necessitate changing a few tiles. It has a real wow factor when you're touring the building. At the moment, it's one of the areas that we only ever visit when we're giving someone the grand tour as we have so much else to do, I can't imagine we'll ever get round to utilising this floor in our lifetimes – but you never know.

The third section of the building needs almost total renovation and is comparatively smaller than the other sections. It has a lot of charm but needs a lot of work, and I have dreams of converting this one day into a two/three-bedroom house and maybe moving into this section of the building when we are older and want something more manageable. It's separated from the rest of the house at the back by the canal and has its own garden which is a strip of land edged either side by the canal and the river. It is the prettiest part of the whole property and is covered in wildflowers in the spring. The strip opens out and then slopes down to where the canal and the river meet which is a truly magical place – so cool, shady and peaceful, it's one of my favourite parts of the grounds. The children paddle here in the summer and play in the water, and the dogs (and kids) like to go for a dip in the river when it's really hot – I've never attempted it as it's much too cold for me.

I hope you can visualise the enormity of the building and the size of project we had taken on. I think most people thought and probably still think we were mad to buy it without the 100,000 euros needed to fully renovate the property, but we always knew it would be at least a ten-year project... we've now been here over 15 years and whilst we have done an enormous amount of work, there is still much to do.

One of the first major projects on the list was the electricity. We hadn't realised before we moved just how bad the electrics were. Gary can turn his hand to most things, but the electrical system here is very different and if we were going to rent out the apartments, we needed to get it done professionally. We didn't have a clue where to start, so a friend recommended a Scottish electrician called Paul who lived quite close to us. We needed the entire house rewired, which is no mean feat and our electric wattage needed to be increased.

The electricity system in France takes a bit of getting used to. We couldn't understand why every time we put our kettle on when the washing machine was on, the electrics tripped. It transpired that we had 9KW of electricity on a *triphase* system and each phase could have a maximum of 3KW, so basically if a washing machine runs on 1.5kw and the kettle takes up 1.8KW and they are both on the same phase, then your electric will blow if they are both on at the same time because you're using more than 3KW! In England you never have to think about how many kilowatts you are using, because it's a ring main system. You can put on as many things as you want and it will never blow unless there is a problem with one of the appliances or the wiring. The system here takes some getting used to, but we are much more aware now of our electricity consumption and always look for appliances with lower KW when we are buying anything new. We had our electric upped to 15KW (5 KW per phase), but it still trips out if we've got too many gadgets on at once. It normally only happens now when we have guests staying in the *gîtes* and they have everything on at the same time.

Paul the electrician was working on our electricity for about three months – it is a huge building and we needed a separate box for each *gîte.* He called in his friend Patrice to help with the more complex task of setting up the *délesteur* which is basically a computer which cuts the supply to certain appliances to stop the electricity from tripping. It works to a point, but only for the things that are put onto the computer – which for us were the heaters in the *gîtes.* At night for example, if there is too much draw on the electricity, then the heaters in the living rooms will cut out and during the day the heaters in the bedrooms will cut out. There were a lot of calculations to get the balance right between the three phases as we had three electric water heaters which were a big draw and three electric hobs. Patrice had to reconfigure the electric hobs, because they were designed for a *monophase* (single phase) which meant if all four rings were put on at the same time it would overload the phase, so he had to split them over three phases. This was all carried out over the very cold months of December, January and February and Patrice and Paul would have lunch and sometimes dinner with us, as they often worked until 8pm, to get the work done. They did a fantastic job, but it unfortunately took virtually all our money allowed for renovation, which was a much smaller budget than we had originally intended. The exchange rate had gone against us at the time of our purchase, from when we had initially started the process and we ended up with about 20,000 euros less than we had planned. It wouldn't have been such a rush, but our first guests had booked in to arrive for the February half term holiday. Some friends/neighbours of ours in England who had kept in touch and were keen to see what we were up to. They also fancied having a go at skiing and as we were only an hour from the slopes, they decided to be our first paying guests. It was good because it gave us a focus and timescale to get the *gîtes* to some sort of habitability before they arrived.

During the electricity works, Gary was working his way through the other list of jobs which included:

- Tiling the floors of the two apartments and the corridor (a total floor coverage of about 250m^2), tiling two bathroom walls and two kitchens
- Plaster-boarding ceilings and walls

- Taking out two bathrooms and replacing them with two kitchens
- Building several cupboards
- Putting in connecting doors

It's incredible, now I look back on it, how he managed to do such an astonishing amount of work in the first six months. It was all largely on his own, although a cousin of his came out and helped a lot. I was out of action on helping physically with the renovating work, as apart from being very occupied looking after the children and the household, I was heavily pregnant. I may not have carried out any of the physical work, but I was very active in helping with deciding on the order of works, materials used, etc. It seemed an impossible task, but miraculously with some help from friends and family, we were ready for guests in June 2005.

Our main project in the second year was to get our third apartment ready on the second floor and to help achieve this we asked my cousin Ginny and her partner Jeff to help. Jeff and Ginny had moved to France at the same time as us, but they decided to go to Brittany. We had been regularly in touch with them and Jeff (who is a builder by trade), offered to come down and help us. As usual we had a deadline to work to – guests were booked in to stay in the *gîte* in June 2006 and we still had a long way to go, but luckily with the help of Jeff and a lot of hard work putting in the finishing touches the night before the guests arrived, we were ready by the skin of our teeth, as we always are.

As our second year came to a close, we started the enormous task of rendering the front of the building. This was no mean feat – the front of the building is approximately 35m long by 15m high. Our neighbours said the previous owner had been quoted about 40,000 euros to have the work carried out by one company – not a sum we could consider. However, it really needed doing as it was a patchwork of crumbling old render, stone and brick where two new floors had been added to the building probably sixty years before and they had just left the bare brick. It looked a total mess.

By this time Gary had given up his job in the UK and so was here permanently and had the time to devote to doing this project. It was very daunting as Gary had rendered small walls before but nothing of this size and he wasn't entirely sure what mix to use, etc. As luck would have it, we had some guests stay with us for a week at the end of August, a few weeks before Gary had planned to carry out the work. The guy had lived in Provence for ten years and his business was carrying out lime renders on buildings. He recommended the exact mixes that Gary should use – how many layers and what additives he should use. It was an enormous help and excellent advice, as fourteen years on it still looks as good as the day he did it.

We really should have hired a scaffold to cover the whole of the building, but we knew that this would be very costly and money was tight, so we borrowed a small scaffold from a friend and had to keep moving it as each section was finished. It was a very long process and a mucky job – lime is not a good substance to work with and can burn your skin and your nostrils if you're not careful.

Another good tip the builder had for Gary was to put Vaseline around his nostrils to stop the lime particles getting up there – a piece of advice he found invaluable. We were very fortunate too that we had a couple renting one of our *gîtes* for six months while they were in the process of buying a house down the road. He was a plumber by trade but was currently not doing anything and so very kindly offered to help Gary with the work. So, the two of them set about this enormous task and made a lovely job of it – it took six weeks to complete but was well worth it, as it completely transformed the whole look and feel of the building. It was an incredible achievement by both and was the largest task we had undertaken at that time.

A family moving to France

Moulin d'en Bas 2020

What's up Doc?

One of the biggest concerns when moving abroad is the health system. Is it good and how much does it cost? Difficult to answer this in a nutshell, so all I can do is share with you our experiences here in France with a sprinkling of comparisons to the UK and let you decide for yourself.

Falling ill, visiting the doctors and taking lots of medication seems to be a national pastime in rural France (a bit like how the British love to talk about the weather). They are certainly not afraid of a trip to the local surgery and are prepared to sit for hours chatting in the doctors waiting room. They'll happily discuss their ailments in the minutest detail with the doctor who is equally happy to sit and chat with them. Everyone expects to come away with a bucket full of medication and the doctors dutifully oblige.

Although the health service is not free in France, if you are legally resident and contributing to the system you are entitled to a certain percentage paid for by the social fund. The first thing you need is a *carte vitale* (health card)– this enables you to have 60-70% of your medical bills paid by the social fund. If you have a chronic illness such as diabetes or a heart problem that is permanent, you are entitled to 100% medical coverage on anything related to that condition. Most people buy a top-up insurance for the balance or pay the difference themselves (not advisable). The cost of top-up insurance or *mutuelle* as it's called in France, depends on the number and age of family members. To get a *carte vitale* you need to be in employment, salaried, self-employed or retired and over the national retirement age. If you are salaried your employer will normally provide the *mutuelle*. If you're entitled to a *carte vitale*, then it will cover you for your dependents too (i.e., spouse and dependent children).

One of the first things I needed to sort on the official side, was getting into the system for health, etc. I'd read all the books before moving but was still confused about where to start. However, I had the good fortune of meeting someone very early on, who proved to be an enormous help to me. We had only been here a few weeks, I was waiting outside Ryan's school, and a heavily pregnant women waddled up to me.

"Hello, are you the Ryan's mother? I'm Marie, my daughter is in his class". She was French but spoke perfect English. She worked for a big company in Toulouse and was on maternity leave as her fourth child was due to be born the following month. We immediately hit it off. She took me under her wing and helped me with so many things. Firstly, she took me to the *CAF (Caisse d'allocations familiales)*, where she helped me register for the *allocation familial* (family allowance). At the time, Gary was working in the UK, so we were still entitled to family allowance from England. I hadn't realised that because we were now permanently resident in France, we were entitled to a monthly payment of the difference between the family allowance in England and the French *allocation familiale*. It amounted to about 300 euros a month at the time, so well worth it. The French system is very encouraging of larger families in an attempt to boost the population. If you have only one child there is not much help, but the more children you have, the more generous the allowance. Also, as I was pregnant, I was entitled to *prime à la naissance* which was then (in 2005) a payment of 750 euros, during the seventh month of the pregnancy, to help buy the essentials for the new baby.

Gary was working in the UK when we arrived and so we were paying tax there. We got forms from the department for Work and Pensions in the UK stating our circumstances, which we handed over the *CPAM (Caisse primaire d'assurance maladie)* here in France which is the equivalent of the Social Security in the UK. I was given a contact in Toulouse to send all our medical forms for reimbursement. We had to pay for the doctors, medicine and specialists during the visit, they would then give me a form which I sent off to Toulouse to claim the money back. I was worried when I went into hospital to have my fourth child that we'd get a big bill at the end, but we didn't, thank goodness. It was all sorted out behind the scenes.

Once Gary was here permanently and we started a business, we were entitled to a *carte vitale*. I was covered under his name and we got a top up insurance which cost about 140€ a month for six of us at the time. It sounds quite simple, but the system here is notoriously difficult. Some people have no problems at all, and others have years of hassle. It took about a year for our *carte vitale* to come through. They kept asking for all sorts of paperwork to prove our business was legitimate. Apparently, they have problems with people starting false companies just to get into the health system. It was a great day when our *carte vitale* arrived – I finally felt that we were properly sorted and in the system. Unfortunately, my euphoria was fairly short lived. A couple of years later when we changed our business to include the garden centre, our *carte vitale* stopped working. The French system can't seem to cope with anyone having more than one business concern.

The French health service is a strange mixture of the ultra-modern often in the cities and the very basic (thirty years behind the times) in the rural backwaters. I was surprised on my first visit to the local doctors – the surgery was very humble (to put it politely) and situated in a terraced building in a back street of the local town. The only sign that it was a doctor's surgery was a gold plaque on the wall outside. I opened the door and felt I had stepped into a time warp. I found myself in a small, dark, rather shabby room with some old wooden chairs, full of elderly people patiently chatting. I looked around for a reception or receptionist, but there was nothing only two doors, one I presumed lead to the surgery and the second was under a stairway with WC printed on it – I could hazard a guess as to what that was.

On entering, their conversations stopped abruptly, quizzical eyes turned on me and they all politely chimed the usual "Bonjour Madame". I weakly responded, "Bonjour Monsieur, Dame" and tentatively asked if I needed to make an appointment, they just shrugged and shook their heads.

I sat down and nervously waited my turn avoiding eye contact and hoping no one would try to talk to me as I had no idea what they were saying. There was no ticket system, but everyone seemed to know exactly when it was their turn, I just had to make sure I could see when all the original patients had gone in and know to go before anyone who arrived after me. There were about five people in the waiting room when I arrived, so I guessed ten minutes per patient I should have to wait about fifty minutes, oh well, never mind. What an underestimation that was! I discovered that the average consultation seemed to be about thirty minutes and so I had to wait for nearly three hours before I got in to see the doctor. What on earth could they be doing in there that warranted all that time? When I did get in to see her, she was very nice and seemed to have all the time in the world. A stark contrast to the UK, where the doctors are writing out the prescriptions and showing you to the door before you've barely had chance to sit down. She was a plump middle-aged woman in her fifties with short grey hair and a lovely smile – it was like having a chat with your mum. She seemed very caring, concerned and very thorough. I can understand why she was so popular with her patients.

She didn't speak any English but was very patient with me and made sure I understood everything she was saying. At the end of the consultation I paid the fee (22 euros at that time) and she completed a form for me to send off to the CPAM to get the money reimbursed. If you have a *carte vitale*, you give it to the doctor who puts it in a machine. Most of the charge now gets paid automatically and you just pay 30% which is covered by your *mutuelle* (if you have one) and is paid into your bank account about a week later. If you're a bit short of cash, the doctor will usually not mind holding onto the cheque for a week until the money is available.

Things have improved in my local doctors since that first visit back in 2004. My original doctor retired a few years ago and the new doctor now has a smart new surgery in a health centre shared by several doctors and she even has a receptionist! It's mainly appointment only now, but there's still a come in and wait policy "sans rendez-vous" on Saturday mornings.

They seem to prescribe much more medication here in France. Go to the doctor with a sore throat and you'll come back with an *ordonnance* (Prescription) bag full of *medicaments* (medicines). However, I was pleasantly surprised at how they embrace complimentary medicine. When I was suffering from severe stress a few years back (chest pains, memory loss, panic attacks, sleepless nights), I told the doctor I wasn't keen on going the anti-depressant route so she picked up a big book from behind her desk, thumbed through the pages and prescribed a number of homoeopathic medicines. Of course, you're never sure if it's the medicines or I was just learning to cope with the stress, but within a month I was feeling much better. A friend of mine was having some problems with shoulder pain, most probably caused from the physical work she was doing (lots of painting and cleaning). As well as pain killers the doctor prescribed a course of physiotherapy which included massage and hydrotherapy techniques – these alternative treatments are often covered by the *mutuelle*.

Doctors and specialists here tend to err on the side of caution. If you have symptoms of something that could be something more serious, they will always send you for tests to rule it out regardless of cost. In the UK it seems that doctors and specialists are always mindful of costs and are less likely to recommend a costly test if the likelihood of you having that condition is slim. They'll always explore other less expensive avenues first. I think an awful lot of money is wasted in France on unnecessary investigations, but you do at least feel your symptoms are being taken seriously and no stone has been left unturned, which often is not the same in the UK.

I feel generally the service we receive in France is much more thorough in terms of investigation into causes of illness and treatment. The downside of this is that we all pay dearly for this level of care. Social charges are very high and unless you're on a very low income, you have to pay extra for top up insurance.

I know everyone in the UK moans about the NHS, the long waiting lists, the lack of care, the poor facilities, but there are certain aspects of the system that I've come to appreciate more since moving to rural France. The actual systems they have for patient care and continuity of care are generally very good (at least they were when I lived there, but that was back in 2004).

The facilities in the cities like Toulouse are excellent, the experts are well trained, but the after and routine care can be disjointed. I was used to the UK system where you have a family doctor who holds all your family's medical history on a computer system. You get automatic reminders when routine tests, check-ups and inoculations are due – you're even given an automatic appointment which you can change if they're inconvenient. In rural France your records at that time were often kept in an envelope in a drawer and sometimes got misplaced (just like England thirty years ago). Some doctors were more up to date and might have records on a computer, but there was no centralised system at that time (although there is one rolling out now apparently). There were no reminders for anything, no systems to check you'd had all the routine tests and check-ups you should have had from your family doctor. It's down to you to carry your recent blood tests/x-rays and a letter from your doctor to the specialist of your choice. The onus is on the patient to remember everything they've ever had wrong with them and tell this to whatever expert they've chosen to see. I suppose many people might like this and don't like the hospital holding records on them that they never see, but I actually find it quite comforting. I like a reminder that I'm due for a smear test or the kids need a vaccination. I find it difficult to remember when these things are due. There are a lot of us and I'm always so busy that these things often get overlooked unless I get reminded, but maybe I've just got spoilt and lazy.

Having said all this though, I do like the fact that I see the results of any tests I have, everything is transparent, and I have more control and choice over my own health care here in France. I've never had to wait longer than a month for a specialist appointment and the clinics and hospitals in the cities are generally fantastic offering far superior medical care, facilities and equipment than I've ever experienced in the UK. Single or twin rooms, scrupulously clean, comfortable, good food and well-staffed – certainly in the private clinics, but not quite so great in the public hospitals, although still superior to my experiences in the UK.

And baby makes 6

When we were planning the move to France, I hadn't really thought about the possibility of having a baby there. We made lots of plans about what we would do when we moved - renovating the house, creating the holiday home business, growing our own vegetables, keeping animals, running gardening courses but the possibility of having another baby hadn't been considered. It was unusual for me, as I usually try to think of every eventuality. It came as a bit of a shock when I discovered two weeks before the move that I was pregnant with our fourth child. There was so much to think about with a move to a new country, sorting out everything to do with pregnancies and babies just seemed another enormous hurdle to clamber over.

My French friend Marie helped me sort out getting health care for the pregnancy. I had already experienced three pregnancies in the UK, so I knew roughly what to expect, but I was new to France and new to the system and not every country deals with things in the same manner, as I would soon find out.

In England, I knew what to do if I was pregnant. I'd go to the doctor, he would make an appointment for me to see the practice midwife who would sort out all my appointments, hospital booking in, etc. In France, you usually go directly to a gynaecologist and not your family doctor. In England, you may have one appointment during the pregnancy with a gynaecologist (unless you have problems), but other than that, the midwife and family doctor deal with your check-ups. `

In France, you visit a gynaecologist monthly to start with and they provide your care and usually deliver the baby too. Marie advised me not to go to a gynaecologist in our closest town with a hospital. She felt they had been responsible for her miscarrying twins the year before, when they missed some vital information during a routine scan. She recommended that I see her gynaecologist in Toulouse, our nearest major city and about an hour drive. It seemed a long way to go, but as

I had troubles with my third pregnancy, I decided it was better to listen to her advice and see the gynaecologist in a *clinique* in Toulouse.

The clinic I went to was very smart and modern. The gynaecologist's office was well equipped and comfortingly professional – very different to the slightly primitive doctors' surgery in our local town. I was surprised at how much medical intervention there seems to be here in pregnancies and childbirth. May I apologise in advance for the next topic for those of you with a sensitive disposition – I will endeavour to describe the following as delicately as possible.

For example, in the UK, I never had an internal exam during pregnancy until I was at the hospital in labour. The general thought in the UK is that unless there's a problem it's best to have as little physical interference as possible. Whereas, in France, I found that I had an internal examination every visit to the gynaecologist (so at least monthly). When I queried if it was necessary, they said it was to check that the cervix was closed. It wasn't pleasant, but you tend to have to get used to things like that when you're having a baby (and I've had my fair share).

During my first visit, the gynaecologist discussed my previous pregnancies and what method of pain relief I would prefer during the birth. I thought it was a bit early to think about that, but apparently if you opt for an epidural (injection into the spine that gives total pain relief during labour) you have to visit an anaesthetist well before the birth to have blood tests and discuss your medical history to assess your suitability for having it. In the UK, I was always discouraged against having an epidural – after all, isn't it unnatural? Don't you get awful headaches afterwards? Can't it permanently paralyse you? All this had been drummed into my psyche over many years. I was surprised to learn that something between 60 - 80% of women in France have an epidural (*péridurale*) in childbirth and it is very well supervised, researched and safe. After all, as Marie said to me, "If you were going to the dentist to have a tooth pulled out, you would have an injection to take the pain away – why not when you have a baby?". Put like that I couldn't argue with her really and I thought, why not indeed? When in France... So, I agreed to the possibility of having an epidural. If I went through the process, had all the tests and it was established it was safe for me to have one, then I could ask for it during the birth, but if I didn't go through the process, then I wouldn't have the option of having one. I felt it was better to keep my options open.

In the UK, I was used to the midwife sorting out all the necessary scans, booking in the hospital, etc, but here you have to do it yourself. The gynaecologist provides you with a prescription (*ordonnance*) for the ultrasound (*echographie*), epidural (*peridural*) and blood tests (*prises de sang*) and you choose where you want to have your tests and scans and ring up yourself to make your own appointments. For my ultrasound scan, I chose the radiography department within the *clinique* where I would give birth, and I was pleased to find that all was well with the baby. Did I want to find out what sex the baby was? "Oui, merci", but I might have known, it was another boy! Four boys, no chance of buying pink dresses and dollies for me - but I was just pleased he was healthy. I started to really look forward to the birth now. I was a little apprehensive though, as I was having him in France and my French wasn't brilliant – what if there were complications and I didn't understand what was going on? Doubts like this would creep into my mind from time to time, but luckily I was too busy with the other 1001 things I had to do with settling into our new home and country that I didn't have time to really think about it too much.

The pregnancy passed without any major incidences. Our biggest problem was who we would get to watch the children when the labour started. My mother very kindly offered to help, but of course you don't know exactly when babies are going to come – my first two arrived on their due dates, but you never can tell. So, we arranged for her to fly over for two weeks (one week before the baby's due date). She arrived on 6th of May, the day before our wedding anniversary, which meant that Gary and I had the chance to go out for a meal together to celebrate. It was the first time we had dined alone since we had that romantic meal in the "Canard Gourmand" when we signed for the house. On this occasion we went to the local *auberge* and had the famous (around these parts, anyway) cabbage soup (which sounds boring but tastes delicious), goats cheese salad, *maigret de canard* (succulent duck breasts chargrilled and much bigger than any duck I've seen in the UK) and finished off with a crêpes suzettes. It was dancing night and they had a man playing an accordion and singing very traditional French songs. There were lots of older couples, the ladies with sparkly dresses and shoes on, all dancing in the aisles. It was a good atmosphere and rather amusing, but thankfully my condition gave me the excuse not to dance – not really my type of music.

Nearly a week had passed since my mother arrived in France and nothing had happened on the baby front. I was getting a bit worried that he was going to be late and she would have to leave before he arrived. I decided to try and help him along by taking long walks and even tried walking up the steep hill to the village. Sure enough, in the middle of the night on the 13th of May, I was getting some mild pains and my waters started leaking. I rang the hospital and, as we had an hour's drive, they said it was best that we come in. Of course, when I arrived at the hospital in the early hours of the morning everything had stopped, so I tried to get a bit of sleep. As my waters had broken and nothing was happening by 6am, they decided to put me on a drip to induce the labour (I'm sure they wouldn't have considered this so quickly in the UK). Within an hour, I was well into labour and ready for the epidural. The difference it made was phenomenal – having never had one before I didn't really know what to expect. In previous labours, I always tried to have as natural a birth as possible, but usually had an injection of pethidine in my leg when the pain got unbearable. Subsequently, I had previously felt a bit spaced out during and after the births. It doesn't seem to take the pain away, just detaches you from it all. But, this time, after the epidural took effect it was amazing. I was sitting up in bed chatting with Gary and whilst I was aware of the contractions, they no longer gave me any pain at all. For the first time in my life, I was fully aware of what was going on during the birth and was able to enjoy it much more. I could feel when it was time to push, I could push the baby out and not feel that excruciatingly searing pain as the head crowns. In fact, I couldn't feel any pain at all – incredible and I felt great afterwards - not so tired and exhausted. And there he was, my beautiful 8lb baby boy who we decided to name Luc. Luke had always been on our list of names for boys, but we'd never used it for the previous three, so we decided to finally use the name but use the French spelling as he was born and would be living in France. I'm not sure who was more relieved about the success of the epidural, me or Gary. When I was in labour for the first time with Matthew, Gary was very distressed to see me in so much pain during the final stages of the birth. Apparently, I was screaming, swearing and pulling my hair out (what a drama queen) and he was feeling helpless and wanted to help in any way he could. He got hold of my hands and said "Nikki, don't pull out your hair, let me help you, squeeze my hands instead". So, I grabbed hold of his hands and apparently when the next contraction came my fingernails dug in so deep that he was nearly on the ceiling with the pain and has the scars to prove it. He learnt his lesson and kept well clear during the subsequent births!

The stay in the *clinique* was vastly different to my experiences in English hospitals. The rooms are either private or a maximum of two people. I had, for some reason, been given a private room and was a little worried I would be charged extra for it, but to my relief I wasn't. The food was nice, the beds were comfortable, the rooms had en-suite showers and toilets, the nurses were friendly and helpful – it was a very pleasant stay and I wasn't in a rush to go home. It was lovely spending a few days getting to know my baby and getting into a routine before being thrust back into the thick of it at home with housework, kids, dogs and businesses to cope with.

Every parent's nightmare

Our first summer here was great – Gary had three months off work, and we spent the entire time either entertaining our *gîte* guests or making jams and preserves. The weather was hot much of the time and we were all in shorts and flipflops. Lots of barbecues in the evenings and long lunches.

However, there was one day towards the end of that first summer in France we will never forget. It was a hot August day; we were home with all the kids and we had no guests staying at the time. Luc was about three months old. I was having a nap just before lunch and he was in the bed with me. I'd been feeding him and he'd fallen asleep in my arms. Gary called me to say lunch was ready. Luc looked so peaceful and cosy in the bed, I thought it was best not to disturb him. He was not rolling yet, so I didn't think there was any chance he could roll off the bed, but just to make sure I wrapped the duvet around his back (he was lying on his side), so he couldn't roll over onto his back. I went off into the kitchen (the room next door) to have lunch. After lunch I went back to the bedroom to check on Luc.

As soon as I walked in the room, I could tell there was something dreadfully wrong. He was lying motionless face down in the bed. I scooped him up and he lay limp and lifeless in my arms, his lips were blue, his eyes were rolling, and he didn't seem to be breathing. Words can't describe the overwhelming feeling of panic and desperation I had at that moment and the following hours were like a dream. I felt as if an enormous hole had opened up and I was being sucked into it. Everything seemed to be happening in slow motion. I called out to Gary – he must have realised from the tone of my voice that something was dreadfully wrong. He told Matthew and Ryan to keep three-year-old James occupied and he rushed into the bedroom.

We stripped off his baby grow and ran next door to ask for help. They immediately phoned 18 for the *pompiers* (fire brigade). It would have been our instinct to phone for an ambulance, but apparently here the best people to phone are the *pompiers* as they are trained in resuscitation and have all the lifesaving equipment on board. Whereas, the ambulances are run by private companies with trained personnel but without the resuscitation equipment. The wait for the *pompiers* to arrive felt like an eternity but was probably about ten minutes. I spent that time pacing up and down my neighbour's hall, jiggling Luc up and down, patting his back and praying he was going to be OK. He was limp in my arms like a rag doll. I kept repeating over and over "Please don't let him die". It is the worse feeling ever, feeling as though your child's life is slipping away from you and there is nothing you can do but wait.

The *pompiers* arrived and whisked Luc off into the van to resuscitate him. I was a complete mess, crying and shaking uncontrollably. I was mildly aware a doctor arrived, and our village mayor had come to offer his help and support. Within about 10 minutes and after oxygen had been administered, Luc was breathing normally again and back to a more normal, healthy colour. I was so thankful and relieved and couldn't thank the *pompiers* enough for saving his life. It took me some time to get over this experience and it still makes me very emotional whenever I think about it. I'm truly thankful that it was all OK in the end and sometimes wonder how life would have been had the outcome been different...

After the summer, Gary was back to working in the UK one week in three and I was back to coping on my own a lot of the time, and now I had the extra responsibility of a sick baby. When Luc was only eight weeks old (a month before having to call out the *pompiers*) he was diagnosed with bronchiolitis which is the baby form of bronchitis. He had physiotherapy for this. A few months later (in the autumn), he had bronchiolitis again. He was very wheezy, although he didn't seem ill at all, in fact he was very happy and contented. The doctor said he was classed as a "happy wheezer" which pretty much described him down to a T. He had another course of physiotherapy which seems to be the standard method of treating breathing related problems. The paediatrician said it was important I find an expert in baby physiotherapy (or *kinesitherapeute* as they call it here) as it was very specialised. My friend called several different physiotherapists until she found one in our local town, about 25 minutes from our home. I went to see him with Luc and all he seemed to do was place a vibrating machine on his chest and then his back and that was it. I thought it a bit strange and it didn't seem to make any difference to his breathing, but he assured me it was standard practice. About a week or so into the course and Luc didn't seem to be getting better, in fact he seemed to be getting worse. The course of physio was supposed to be carried out on Sundays and bank holidays if necessary. On my appointment on the Saturday he said he'd be fine until Monday, "Are you sure?" I queried. Oh yes, he wasn't worried about him. I felt uneasy, he really didn't seem to be getting better to me. The following morning (Sunday) and he was really bad, temperature and struggling to breathe. I had to take him to the emergency paediatrician in Toulouse. I was on my own with the three children (Gary was away in England) and I had to drive through the centre of Toulouse to find a clinic I'd never visited before with a very sick baby. Stressed was not the word really. Luckily, Ryan was very helpful (eleven years old at the time) and helped me find the right place. It transpired that Luc had developed chickenpox, which whilst not usually dangerous, it was not a good combination with the bronchitis he had. His breathing was very bad, and the doctor arranged for me to have an emergency visit with a specialist baby physiotherapist in another clinic. Luckily, it was Sunday and so the traffic was quite quiet, and parking was reasonably easy. I found the clinic and waited for the physiotherapist to arrive. She was only about mid-twenties she took one look at Luc and tutted.

"How long has he been like this."

"He's been treated for the past week by a physiotherapist in our local town".

"He's not going to like this, but it's necessary" she explained.

She laid him on his back and started really pressing hard on his chest several times, then she brought him upright and managed to push a great stream of phlegm from his mouth. Poor little chap didn't know what had hit him, but I could see she knew exactly what she was doing. This stupid machine that the other physio had used was useless.

He'd never coughed up anything. I decided I had to make an appointment to see her again. Toulouse was over a two-hour round trip every day, but if this is what he needed, then this is what had to be done. Within a few days, he was really starting to improve and within a few weeks, that course of physio was over. Unfortunately, it was not the end of it though. Luc had many episodes over the following months. Many physio visits and a nebuliser machine to help with his breathing when the attack was severe. It was finally diagnosed as asthma and after lots of tests they found he had gastric reflux which was probably the main contributing factor to his asthma. He was given some medication to help with this and gradually over the next year or so his symptoms subsided until they were barely there.

Looking back on it now, I realise that this was probably Matthew's cause of asthma too. For many years I had been carrying the guilt of his asthma attacks being caused by separation anxiety when I had to work when he was young. Matthew still has gastric reflux, but nowadays it just means he has a bit of indigestion if he eats things too acidic – Gary has it too, in fact all of the children have it to some degree or another, it's obviously hereditary. When Matthew was young though, it was never considered a possible cause of asthma, but it makes a lot of sense now.

Thankfully soon after Luc's birth, James' behaviour started to improve. He went from a very difficult and unpredictable child, to a very reasonable, kind and considerate boy. Friends that know him now cannot believe he was so challenging as a small child. Luc was a very placid baby and spent a lot of his time just looking around and taking everything in or dozing (when he wasn't ill). Once he started to walk however, it was a different story. At eighteen months it was like the testosterone had kicked in and he became a wilful and daredevil child and so it continued...

Although I never really felt homesick, the only time I wished I could be in England was when my father had a heart attack. Luc was a baby and all I wanted to do was drop everything and be with him, but I couldn't. Luckily, it wasn't too major. He had a stent fitted and very quickly recovered. The other times I felt homesick were when my nieces got married and I couldn't go to the weddings – it was hard in the early days because money was very tight and the kids were young. Now I can go to the UK if I need to, even at a day's notice (which I've unfortunately had to in more recent years). It makes living life abroad much easier when you can get back to friends and family within a few hours if necessary.

Pendre la Crémaillère

At the end of our first year in France, we had been so busy getting on with life that we hadn't had the time to entertain at all. We decided it was time to start bursting out of our bubble and have a house-warming party (*pendre la crémaillère* or *pendaison de crémaillère*) to celebrate our first year. We knew very few people at the time, just one English couple we'd met through schools, my English-speaking French friend Marie, our electricians and our neighbours. Anyway, despite that, we decided to invite everyone, give them an opportunity to see what work we had done in the *gîtes* and thank them all for their help and hospitality.

So, the invitations went out, we busied ourselves preparing the house and food and about thirty or so guests came along to see what we'd been up to. As people arrived, we greeted them and Gary gave them a tour of the *gîtes*. Most of our neighbours were very familiar with the building and had grown up either living or working in it and had many stories to tell. An old couple up the road told us they had had their wedding reception in our sitting room. There was a lovely friendly atmosphere and I think they appreciated what we were trying to do.

The party started at 3pm and at 5.30 we announced the buffet was ready and would they please help themselves to food. They all looked at us with bemused faces – not only were they not used to eating so early (the French usually dine in the evenings about 7 or 8pm), but they weren't used to a cold buffet and helping themselves. Everyone was seated around the tables laid out in our sitting room so we started handing round the food and serving them, or I don't think anyone would have eaten. At the end of the meal I stood up and made a speech in my best French (thanks to the aid of google translate). Here's a rough translation of what I was trying to say in English:

"Thank you very much everyone for coming here today to celebrate with us our first year in France and *Moulin d'en Bas*.

A family moving to France

First allow me to say 'excuse me' because my French is not very good but I speak a little more than Gary so I must speak for both of us.

When we arrived here, Gary didn't speak any French, but now thanks to M. Gordan he can say 'rock', 'chainsaw', 'electric fence' and other very useful words. I speak a little more, but this year Gary and I must try harder to learn to speak French or we will not be able to understand James!

This year we were very busy. We had a lot of work in the house to finish the *gîtes* and also Luc was born in May. Now we are very pleased to tell you that we have two apartments ready and we also have rooms for us and the boys.

It has been a difficult time for us, but also nice because everyone has been very kind to us. We want to say a big thank you to our neighbours M and Mme Gordan. They have helped us with many things and without their help when Luc had a problem with his breathing, he would not be here today. It is very comforting to know they are there if we need them, especially when Gary is in England and I'm alone with the children. We are very fortunate to have neighbours like this.

M and Mme Delfour too - thank you very much for your help and for fruit and vegetables. Now we have a lot of jam and soup - we will never go hungry this winter!

I must say a big thank you to my friend Marie. I had the good fortune to meet her after we had been here for just three weeks and she has helped with many things - especially with pregnancy. Without her support, life would be much more difficult for us. Thank you very much.

Finally, I would like to say that we are very happy living here. We love our home, the region, the mountains, the food, the wine, the people and the climate. This is a very nice part of France and we hope to be here for many more years.

I hope you have understood everything I've tried to tell you. I've finished now - thank you to everyone and enjoy!"

I'm sure it was largely incorrect, but they all laughed in the appropriate places and really seemed to appreciate the effort. By the end of the evening, we were shattered but pleased so many had come and that we seemed to have done the right thing. We are now accepted as part of the community, never fully French, but our neighbours seemed to appreciate we were making the effort and they forgave us for our eccentricities. We are and will always be *Les Anglais* or in other words "That crazy English family who live in that enormous watermill!"

Living the "Good Life"

O f course it wasn't just the renovating of the house, but also the development of the land which was just as important. Everyone who moves here from the UK tends to want as much land as possible – we are so used to having tiny gardens and land is so expensive and in such short supply that for many of us, the idea of owning some land is very appealing. What we often fail to consider is the enormous amount of time it takes to upkeep land and how quickly it can turn to wilderness if not managed correctly. Gary, having a degree in landscape management, was aware of the amount of time needed in managing the land. After all, it is his profession and, somehow, he managed to find the time to start to organise the land too. It was important for our business to create the right environment to attract guests to stay in our apartments and it was important for us to have some manageable spaces for the animals, vegetables and for the children to play safely.

One of the first jobs we needed to do in the garden was to fence in the dogs. Many dogs in France roam freely, but we didn't feel this was appropriate for our dogs – the St. Bernards in particular are very big and our neighbours seemed wary of them. In order to fence them in, we needed to establish where our boundary was with the neighbour. We have about a 10m gap on one side of our building with our next-door neighbours and we wanted to know where the dividing edge was to work out where to put the fence. When we asked the neighbours, they looked very surprised to even be asked. I think they wondered why we were bothering about that when we had so much land. It's strange but I suppose because land is at such a premium in the UK, we all like to know exactly what is ours and we guard it jealously, but here the same principles don't seem to apply. Most people have lots of land so arguing about where the boundaries are is not normally an issue. However, our neighbours presumed that the delineating edge would be halfway between the two properties (which would make sense), but they were concerned that our fence didn't restrict access for the lorry that comes twice yearly to refill their fuel tank. Of course, we didn't want to upset our neighbours and, yes, we did have lots of land, so we made sure to leave plenty of room for any lorries.

During the first winter we had a very heavy storm one night and several of the trees around the lake fell down. It forced us to tackle this problem as they were too big for Gary to move or deal with alone. Our neighbours put us in touch with some wood fellers who we arranged to come one day and fell lots of the larger trees for us and take them away. They did this for free as they could take the wood and they even paid us for the wood they took. It was great to get the trees thinned as although we had a lot, most of them were poplar and alder, so not very interesting and were overcrowded. Gary went around and marked the trees he wanted to keep with an X and they felled the rest. The woodsmen left an awful mess as they took all the large tree trunks but stripped the trees of the small branches and left them where they fell. Our lake was full of branches and the land was a muddy mess of deadwood and stumps. It took months for Gary to work his way through burning the debris.

Putting in hedges was another job to create privacy for the area we wanted for a barbecue and pool and also around the fenced area for the dogs. The first hedge Gary planted was chopped down by the local SIVOM (council workers) when they came around to do the yearly hedgerow cutting – apparently it was too close to the edge of the road!

Then there were the recreation areas – Gary built a children's play area, put up a plunge pool, created a barbecue area and turned one of the barns into a games room.

One of our main aims in those early years was to become self-sufficient. We'd always wanted to grow our own vegetables and keep animals, and often had in a small way in England, but we never really had the time or the space before to do it properly. Now, we had plenty of space and certainly more time (when Gary wasn't working in the UK or busy renovating). We started off by preparing the vegetable plot – Gary asked our neighbour, a cattle farmer, if he could spare any manure. He brought over about four trailers full of cow manure - he was very happy to oblige. Then once he'd worked it into the land and left it for a while, we were ready for planting. We'd never grown anything on a large scale before, so didn't really know how much to grow. Gary planted out loads of tomatoes, aubergines, courgettes, beans, leeks, peppers, cucumbers and sweetcorn. Within a few months we were inundated with veg – we had no idea it would so fruitful. We had so much that a friend of mine used to take the excess into work with her to sell at the company where she worked in Toulouse. Organically grown vegetables from the country are very popular. We also left piles of vegetables on the table in the entrance for the guests to help themselves to. We had dozens and dozens of tomatoes and I made tons of tomato passata by chopping the tomatoes up and cooking them until they softened, separating out the seeds and the peel with a *mouli*, then pouring the remaining mixture into bags and freezing. It kept us right through until the next summer. Gary also made a drying box out of an old bedside cabinet from Emmaus for 5 euros – he made several shelves with holes and put a light bulb in the bottom. He then cut up and salted tomatoes and put them in the box to dry. This worked extremely well and within a few days we would have dried tomatoes which are excellent for adding to sauces, soups, etc. We had mountains of vegetables and I learnt 100 ways to cook a courgette. We had courgette soup – very nice with *crème fraîche* and grated cheese, ratatouille, courgette gratin, stuffed courgettes, courgette jam – you name it, we made it. The kids were sick to death of courgettes by the end of the summer. "What's for lunch Mum? Oh no, not courgette gratin again" and then at teatime it would be, "Oh no, please, not another ratatouille". I must admit, it did get a bit tedious after a while, but all the same, I missed them once they were gone. Then we'd get a crate full of delicious black figs from our generous neighbour Monsieur Delfour, with which, after we'd eaten our fill, we would make jam and pickle.

One of our visitors had once given us a recipe for fig chutney, which is the most delicious chutney ever, and we make it every year without fail. When we first moved to France we didn't miss much about the food, but we did crave for Branston Pickle. However, since discovering this delicious recipe, Branston no longer makes it onto our wish lists of goodies to ask for when we have visitors from the UK.

Fig Chutney

1.5 kg black figs quartered (or any figs can be used)
1 kg sugar
3 onions chopped roughly
500g mixed raisins and sultanas
1 lt good quality red wine vinegar
2 teaspoons cayenne pepper
2 teaspoons paprika
2 teaspoons ground ginger
2 teaspoons all spice
2 tablespoons chilli sauce (sweet or not up to you!)
6 garlic cloves crushed
salt and pepper

Place all ingredients together and bring to the boil, then simmer for two hours until good chutney consistency (whatever that is).
Pour into jars. This chutney gets better with age apparently, although we have never had it long enough to find out!

Pumpkins are also excellent value – I love spicy pumpkin soup or roasted pumpkin with garlic and olive oil and not forgetting pumpkin pie. Then in the autumn when the air starts getting cooler and damper in the mornings and evenings it's time to hunt out the mushrooms. Our neighbour showed us the best places to get *trompettes de la mort*, *chanterelles* and *pieds-de-mouton*. It's great fun hunting for mushrooms with the kids, then cooking up a tasty omelette for lunch. Monsieur Delfour, our neighbour, had been careful to show us exactly what we should look for as a mistake can be deadly. It's extremely rewarding growing, harvesting, cooking and preserving your own vegetables and of course they taste so much better. It is time consuming though, but well worth the effort. If you find some wild mushrooms but are not sure if they are safe to eat, it is said you can take them to the local pharmacy for identification (although a friend of ours tried and their pharmacy couldn't help).

We also had a menagerie of animals – chickens, ducks, goats, sheep and pigs. It was our intention to eat the animals and we did eat some of the chickens and the ducks, but we never really enjoyed it and in fact several years later we all have become vegetarians. Apart from the fact that we had reared these animals before we killed, plucked and roasted them, because they were free range, they were very muscular, so also rather tough. The goats (Greta and Heidi) were never meant to be eaten – they were only there to keep down the weeds. We took them to the local goat farmer to leave with his herd for a few days to try to get them pregnant as we liked the idea of having goats' milk and making cheese. Unfortunately (or fortunately you could say under the circumstances), they didn't get pregnant, however, I did (not by the goat or the goat farmer of course). So, it was just as well the goats didn't have kids as we wouldn't have been able to cope with the milking as I was too busy with my own!

In addition to the two goats we had for clearing the land, we were given two pigmy goats as pets. We thought they would be nice for the kids, and the visitors. We named them Samson and Delilah. Samson was black and white and very stocky with pink eyes that made him looked demon like. He was very smelly, that really strong goat smell, as he was constantly marking his territory everywhere and particularly over himself. He was small (well he was a dwarf), but he was really bold and full of himself. He was like one of those little yappy Jack Russells that bark and bite a lot to make up for the fact that they're so small. In fact, he took to charging at anyone who got near him – so much for being a nice pet for the kids! Luc was about two at the time and he was absolutely fearless. He is what my mother calls "all boy". There is nothing even remotely feminine about him – he was in the front of the queue when they were handing out testosterone. When he started walking at just over one year old, he didn't just walk, he swaggered like John Wayne! Are you getting the picture? This is one tough little boy! We were all frightened to go in the pen with Samson, but Luc just used to roll up to the pen, pick up a big stick and would run at him with it and Samson never bothered him, but he would terrorise everybody else!

We bought two piglets, one black and one pink, which we called Penny (black) and Babe (how original) and two sheep we called Kylie and Sheila. They were very young when we got them and we had to feed them bottles of milk regularly in the beginning, which was really nice for the children, and they all loved it. We had intended eating the pigs, but they never got big enough. We had accidentally bought a dwarf variety and I'm not sure we could have eaten them anyway. It's difficult not to get attached to them, still, we had every intention of doing it though.

Oh dear, oh deer

We had some friends come to visit one evening who had a holiday home in a nearby village. They left about midnight and about half an hour later we were getting ready to go to bed when there was a knock at the door. Gary went down to see who it was and there were our friends Chris and Julia on the doorstep.

"I'm sorry to trouble you again Gary, but we've had a bit of an accident", said Chris and he took Gary over to the car and opened the boot. Inside was a young deer – dead of course.

"I didn't know what to do with it as we're off back to England tomorrow, but I thought you and Nikki might like it".

"Yes of course, thank you". So, he and Chis carried the deer upstairs and placed it on the kitchen table. They said their goodbyes again and we shut the door and went back to the kitchen and stared at it. There was this beautiful animal lying lifeless on our kitchen table.

"Poor thing. What are we going to do with it?" I asked puzzled.

"Well, we'll have to cut it up and store it", replied Gary. "It's a shame it's dead, but it seems a waste not to." I supposed he was right, but I wasn't overly enthused about the idea. We didn't know where to start. If we were going to do it, we had to do it straight away, as I didn't want the children coming down in the morning and seeing it there. So, I got on the Internet and googled "How to butcher a deer". It's amazing what you can find on the Internet. I found lots of information and printed out some suitable instructions with pictures. Gary sharpened up some knives. The whole idea of what we were about to do just totally turned my stomach, but I told myself not to be so stupid. It's just an animal that's dead. I was a meat-eater at that time, so I felt if I was prepared to eat meat I ought to be able to prepare the meat I eat. It was not even as if we had killed the deer – it was an accident, so I didn't have the guilt of that. I managed to talk myself into being very methodical about it and not to think about what it had been.

Gary strung it up from the beams in the kitchen (which wasn't an easy task as it was very heavy) and proceeded to skin it. The skin came off much easier than I had imagined and peeled off in one go. He then gutted it (which was the worst part and smelt awful). Then he laid it out on the table while I studied the diagrams and we worked out between us where he should cut the various joints. Once I had detached myself from the fact of what it was we were butchering, I was surprised to find it actually quite interesting to see exactly where all these different cuts came from. The sirloin, the belly joint, the shoulder, etc. I'd never really thought about this before. Gary cut them and I labelled the bags and stored them either in the fridge or the freezer. It took hours, but we had to get it done and cleared away before the children came down in the morning. It was not something I wanted our young children to witness - I didn't think the little ones were old enough to understand and I didn't want them having nightmares. So, by about 4am we were finished and then crawled off to bed to get a couple of hours sleep before the dawn wake up of Luc and James jumping on our bed. The next day we had barbecued deer and, although I wouldn't find it so today, at the time it was simply delicious.

Mes amis

The first year or so in France was all about renovating and developing our *gîtes*. On a personal front, I was coping with settling our children into school, pregnancy and getting to grips with having a new baby in a new country. We didn't really have time to develop any sort of social life outside of our immediate family and neighbours as we were too busy coping with day to day living. However, as things started to settle and we began to feel more at home with our new surroundings, we decided it was time to do something about our virtually non-existent social life.

The French are very friendly, and we had formed some good friendships, but it's difficult when you're not a fluent speaker. Also, the local French are quite difficult to get close to. They're friendly and polite, but don't often open their homes to outsiders. Even the French who move here from other parts of France say they find it difficult to make friends locally. In many cases, the local French treat their own countrymen (who've moved to the country from the city) with more suspicion than us foreigners. We didn't initially have intentions to come to France and seek out the English-speaking community, but after a while you tend to crave a conversation in English. You long for the chance of not having to think about everything you say and not having to struggle to understand what's being said. We had come to the point where we felt we needed some more interaction. It was time to branch out, find new people and socialise.

It was around this time when we discovered Angloinfo which was an information website for English speakers, and it had a forum for lots of different areas in France (as well as many other countries popular with 'expats'). There was a wealth of information here and the forum was very useful for anything from buying and selling second-hand items to finding out how to get a *carte vitale*.

One day I saw a post from Heather who had recently moved here with her husband and son (who was a little older than Luc). She was pregnant and feeling lost as to where to start. I got in touch with her, having just been through the entire pregnancy process here, and we met up. She lived about fifty minutes away in the foothills of the Pyrenean mountains, but fifty minutes seemed perfectly reasonable to drive to speak to someone going through the same experiences as yourself in your own language. Shortly after that, Zoe put up an ad to meet up with other mums, she was only about fifteen minutes away from me and had three children, a little older than James and Luc, two boys and a girl. She joined Heather and I and we advertised for more mums to join us. Within a year there were about fifteen of us who regularly met up at each other's houses within a 50-minute radius. It was so great to be able to talk through our problems, share some laughs and it was good for the children too. It was difficult to socialise in the evenings because we all had young children, but we all looked forward to our regular meet ups. Some of the friends I made then, I'm still friends with now, some I rarely see because fifty minutes is quite a long way when you are busy running a business and your kids are at school. About 60% of them have now moved back to the UK for one reason or another. Those meetings really helped me; I'd forgotten how much I missed not having friends. It's important to find your tribe and although Gary doesn't seem to need friends as much as I do, we needed to have some sort of social life outside of the home.

I'm very much a believer in "Everything comes to those who wait", but when it comes to socialising and making friends, you really have to make the effort. Friends don't often just appear by chance, especially if you're not going anywhere you might meet anyone. You have to make the effort, join a local club, join a language course, etc. This was quite difficult for us with the children. Gary was busy working on the house and I had no one to help with babysitting, so what could we do?

We decided, since we found it difficult to join a group, that we'd start our own gardening club and run it from our home. Gary's French wasn't good enough to teach in French, so it would have to be for English speakers. I mentioned it to a friend who was working as an estate agent at the time. She was really enthusiastic about it and very encouraging. She had many contacts within the English community and was sure it would be popular. Had it not been for her encouragement, we probably wouldn't have started it. How can you start a club when you know no one? So, we decided to give it a go. I wrote some flyers advertising it which I forwarded to her and we leafleted all the houses I knew in the area which were English owned. I also put an ad on the website Angloinfo. Our first meeting was held in our barn in Spring 2006. I was so worried that no one would turn up to that first meeting, but it seemed that there was a fair amount of interest and we had a respectable turnout –about twelve people. This grew over subsequent years to about forty members. We met once a month and Gary would give a talk around a specific topic, plus he led a discussion with question and answer sessions on seasonal jobs in the garden. Every year we organised a barbecue and vegetable competition in the summer and a quiz night and meal in the winter. We had a strong core membership who were supportive of all the events we organised, and we formed lots of close friendships as a result. Notably, a couple we met through the first meeting of the garden club (who became great friends) coincidentally moved into a house the other side of our village at the same time as us in 2004. Remarkably, we had never met, despite living in the same village for nearly eighteen months - that shows how little we went out!

Earning a living

One of our main concerns when moving to France was what we were going to do to make a living. We weren't of retirement age and although we had enough equity in our property in the UK to buy a house outright in France there was nothing left over, and we had no other form of income. Gary's profession at the time was as a horticultural lecturer and I was an IT trainer – there was no chance of us getting similar jobs in France, as neither us spoke French well enough. Gary continued lecturing in the UK for the first 18 months, but it was never our intention that he would continue doing this permanently. We had run a guest house for the last three years in the UK, in tandem with our teaching jobs and whilst we had enjoyed it, we found that it was extremely tying. Our days were filled with breakfasts, cleaning, evening meals and waiting for guests to arrive. It wasn't an easy business with young children either. The *Moulin* did lend itself nicely to be a *chambre d'hôtes* (Bed and Breakfast). In fact, I think a previous owner had this in mind because he had started converting bedrooms with ensuite bathrooms. However, we decided that we didn't want to be tied down to breakfasts and evening meals anymore and whilst there is no doubt that *chambre d'hôtes* would be more profitable, we preferred to offer self-catering holiday apartments or *gîtes*. That way we would only need to be there to see them in when they arrived and do the cleaning on changeover days.

We were aware that there are a lot of *gîtes* available, so we had to think how we could attract people to come and stay in our apartments. The other thing was that they were not self-contained houses with a private garden, but holiday apartments with a shared garden and recreational areas, so we had to have something a bit different to appeal to people. We decided to make our holiday apartments 'family friendly' and having children of our own was a big selling point for families. We know from our own experience that it's difficult to find the right holiday when you have children, especially if you like a quiet life. If you find a nice relaxing place, that's all very well, but if the children aren't happy, there's no way they'll let you relax. So our main selling points were: beautiful surroundings in an old Watermill with fishing lake, canal and river frontage, reasonable prices with comfortable accommodation, children's play area with swings, splash pool, games room, bikes available for hire, barbecue area, owners on site with several children of varying ages, animals and organic fruit and vegetables grown on site with homemade jams and pickles available.

We considered registering and getting a grant with "*Gîtes de France*" but found that the rules and regulations were so stifling we decided it was better to go it alone. I set up a website for the *gîtes* and researched the best places to advertise and away we went. We didn't register the *gîtes* as a business as such, because you didn't have to at the time if it wasn't your main income, under 23,000 euros a year, and if you had five beds or less. The income was simply declared on our tax returns at the end of the year as income earned from property and there is an allowance on the income you are taxed which was about 23%.

The advertising paid off and we had a good first couple of seasons with many families from Ireland and Australia. We would often host barbecues for the guests and most evenings were spent sitting outside drinking wine and chatting while the guests' kids played happily with our kids well into the night. We'd created a relaxed and carefree atmosphere and the visitors loved it. They would often complain that their kids were so happy playing around here that they found it difficult to get them away to go on visits to anywhere else.

During our second year (in 2006) Gary gave up his lecturing job in the UK as commuting was becoming unbearable. The income from the *gîtes* wasn't really enough, so we started running gardening courses in the quieter periods. We ran short four- or five-day residential courses on topics like 'garden design' or 'organic gardening' and a few two-day courses for locals. They proved very popular and we would have loved to continue with them, but our growing family made it extremely difficult: I just didn't have the time to manage it all properly and after the second set of courses in the Spring of 2007 we had to shelve that project for some time. Now the children are older, we have started them again.

Our original idea of running *gîtes* and being self-sufficient, whilst a bit of a cliché, was really enjoyable, but unfortunately not sustainable for a family our size. The *gîtes* turned out to be far more seasonal than we had expected, and we had more children than we had originally planned. Self-sufficiency was a lovely dream and something we continue to dabble with and are returning to now that the kids are older. Within a couple of years of moving here though, it became apparent we needed to find another source of income.

One thing we've found is that living here you have to be flexible to earn a living. In the UK when we had our guest house, we used to host French students. I remember saying to Gary how good it would be if we could do the same in France. When Luc was about six months old, I saw an advert on Angloinfo advertising for English families to host French students in France. It turned out to be the same company we had worked for in England. I contacted them and spoke to the owner. It seemed she was looking for a representative in our area to work as a coordinator, visiting potential families to determine their suitability and then placing students with appropriate host families. It was working on a self-employed basis and whilst it wasn't loads of money (it basically covered expenses) it would not take up much of my time and would be an ideal opportunity for me to get out and meet people too. It was perfect and I jumped at the chance. Not only was it my job to find suitable families, but we also hosted too, so much of our summer months were taken up with entertaining *gîte* guests and hosting (and teaching) French students. It worked really well generally and suited our lifestyle at the time.

The income from the students helped, but it still wasn't enough to cover our increasingly growing living costs. We had to think of something else and landscaping was the obvious choice. It was something Gary knew inside and out having run a landscaping business for many years in England and he was good at it. Horticulture was his profession and his passion. He was reluctant to start though as it felt a bit of a step backwards, but needs must. He started off just working a few days a week, trying to keep it fairly low key, but it soon developed into a full-time job.

Accidents will happen

UNfortunately, we've had many experiences with accidents and emergencies whilst living in France. Some have been positive considering the circumstances, some not so positive.

Accident and emergency services at hospitals vary. I have heard a few good reports about our local ones, but I've heard more bad than good. The average waiting time, whenever we have been, seems to be three to four hours. A few years back I had the misfortune to test the service for myself. We had a barbecue (as we often do in the summer) and I must have been bitten by something that evening as the next day I awoke to pains in my thigh. Throughout the day the pains were getting worse and the pain started shooting right down to my foot. In the afternoon my foot started to swell (where I'd been bitten) and I was feeling feverish and faint. If I sat down, I felt OK, so I just thought it was probably an allergic reaction and I'd just leave it to run its course. However, in the early evening (when the doctors' surgeries were closed) I had dark purple streaks running up my inner thigh and started to panic.

"Gary, look at this" I showed him my thigh. "I think I'd better go to the hospital and get this checked out"

"Well, you've got plenty of petrol in the car, I've filled it up for you today, so you'll be OK".

"Ermm, my foot is really painful, and I've got a temperature and feel faint and dizzy – I can't drive myself, you'll have to take me". Can you believe men sometimes! Anyway, we rang someone to come over to watch the children (it was about 8pm and nearly time for bed) and we set off for our local hospital. We arrived at 8.30pm to a full waiting room. The reception was closed and there was not a member of staff in sight. We rang the bell and sat down. No one came. After about 30 minutes Gary decided to find someone. He went through the doors and into the examining area. Apparently, there were lots of people just standing around a bed laughing and joking.

"Can someone come and see my wife, she's very ill", he said.

125

"Bientôt" (soon) was the response.

Thirty minutes later and Gary rang the bell again. A girl in a white coat came out. "Do you speak English",

"A little",

"My wife has been poisoned; she's very ill and needs to see a doctor". I waited on the hard metal waiting room seats feeling queasy, hot outside, cold inside. I just wanted to lie down and go to sleep. She took my name, address and date of birth and that was it. She didn't ask me any questions, didn't take my temperature, didn't check my blood pressure or take my pulse. A few hours later she came out and called a few names – there was no response.

"Il est mort" (he's dead) Gary shouted out. I don't think she was amused. At 11.30pm, after three hours of waiting I was finally shown into the examining room. I could have died in that time and it felt as though no one would have noticed or cared – just one less patient to see! The examining room was small and poorly equipped. The floor was dirty and there were cracks in the lino around the edges of the floor harbouring thick crusts of dirt (and god knows what else). The paintwork was chipped, and it was in dire need of some decorating.

I explained my symptoms to the nurse. She looked at my swollen, red, hot foot and said "Does it normally look like that"

"Ummm, no!"

She took my temperature (which had gone down by now) and my blood pressure and pulse were ok, so that was good. I was asked to wait and about ten minutes later a young girl came in (about mid-twenties I would think) and said she was the covering doctor. I think she was a trainee, as she didn't seem to know very much. After examining me and going off several times for advice, it was concluded that I had an infection, which had travelled through the lymphatic system in my leg. I was given antibiotics, pain killers and sent home and I was thankfully much better within a few days. I'm still not sure what caused it; possibly a horse fly or it could also have been a snake bite as one doctor suggested. We will probably never know....

Ironically, the following day while I was resting my foot at home, Gary received a call from the school – James who was about six at the time had fallen and cut his head open and needed stitches. "Oh no, not another trip to accident and emergency" was Gary's response (after checking James was OK of course). He had to leave work and pick him up. He decided to seek the advice of the local doctor first, the three hours of waiting in accident and emergency only hours before, still painfully vivid in his mind. The doctor's waiting room was the complete opposite. After five minutes of waiting the doctor saw him ahead of the old lady who had been waiting before him. "You have two options – you can take him to the hospital to get stitches or I can clamp his head here and glue it". A no brainer really - Gary opted for the glue, which was all over in five minutes. If only all ailments could be fixed like this. However, James does still have a little bald patch where it was glued. Luckily, he has such thick hair it can't be seen.

Another memorable experience of the accident and emergency services was after a trip to England for my sister's fiftieth birthday party. On the way back to Southwest France, we decided to make a detour to our cousins in Brittany. After all, it's sort of on the way home isn't it? WRONG! It was actually more than a 600km detour. Still, my parents were travelling with us in their campervan with my brother and cousin – it would be fun. I was travelling in a car with three little ones in the back (aged nine, six and three) and Ryan (seventeen) was in the front. We followed the campervan – it was a bit slow, but we'd decided to stick together until lunchtime and then I'd speed off in my Mercedes and get there quicker. Within about 45 minutes my Dad pulled over into an *aire* and I followed. My cousin Ginny was feeling sick. They thought it was the fumes from the hydrogen converting contraption my Dad had set up in the back of the camper to reduce fuel consumption (don't ask). It was decided that it was better that Ginny travel with me, and Ryan (my very capable and sensible son) travel with them in the camper. The reasoning was it would be a more comfortable ride for Ginny (reclining leather seats, air con, etc.) and we could get her home quicker. It should be said at this point that

Ginny had a serious operation earlier that year and was still recovering from the effects of it.

So, off we set again, complete with some plastic "sick" bags provided by my Dad "just in case". Well, within five minutes the inevitable happened and I've never heard or seen anything like it. It kept the kids quiet - they just sat wide-eyed while we all tried to ignore the fact that poor Ginny was chucking her guts up. I pulled over at the next *aire* for her to sort herself out – unfortunately the sick bags had safety holes in, so she was covered in drips of bright yellow vomit. After about ten minutes she said she'd be okay, although she didn't look okay. In the meantime, we had lost sight of the camper van, they must have passed by without seeing us pull over into the *aire*. I was starting to wonder if it had been such a great idea, to leave me alone with a sick adult and three small children, but it was too late now.

So, off we set again, after a few minutes of silence Luc piped up "Pooh that smell is making me feel sick". "Don't talk about it, you'll get me going again" said Ginny and sure enough off she went again.

We passed a sign for a hospital on the motorway and I started thinking "shall I make a joke about taking her there", but then thought better of it - it didn't feel like the time for jokes. A bit further on and Ginny said, "I'm sorry Nikki, but I think you're going to have to take me to that hospital".

Oh my God, I thought, but I didn't say it out loud. "OK" I said trying my best to stay calm, but the signs for the hospital had disappeared, so we must have passed the turn off. I pulled over at the next *aire* – it was one of those with only a toilet and a telephone. I parked the car and ran out towards the telephone and as I looked back, I saw Ginny stagger out of the car and collapse on the grass at the side of the road. Oh dear – I didn't know which way to turn. I decided it was best to call for the *pompiers* first. But I'd no idea where I was as hadn't been paying attention to the signs (one of the many problems with satnavs). There was no mention in the telephone box of where we were either (how useful). I desperately tried to explain "I'm about an hour from Dunkirk on the motorway".

"Which direction are you heading" they asked.

"Towards Brittany" I replied. Well that whittles it down then! Luckily a guy in a van arrived to service the toilets and I got him to speak to the *pompiers* and explain where we were.

I went back to Ginny who was lying on the grass moaning, "Please hurry up, when are they coming?" I told her they were on their way and should be here soon. Luckily an English couple had stopped to help, and the lady was talking to Ginny while I ran around after the little ones, who had got bored by this point. I tried phoning my Dad to come and help, but there was no reply on his mobile. Then, the heavens opened, and it started pouring with rain and the two youngest started jumping up and down in the puddles. The lady had a brolly and gave Luc the job of holding the umbrella over Ginny - good idea to give him a responsibility, why didn't I think of that? The *pompiers* took ages - after twenty minutes they still weren't there. The service man phoned them again. The kind lady looked at me and said, "What about you, are you alright?" Not the best question to ask me at that particular moment.

"No, not really", was all I could reply, the tears started to well up and a few dropped, then I pulled myself together - this was not the time for self-pity! So, there we were standing in the pouring rain, still waiting for the *pompiers* and Ginny moaning on the floor - by this time the service guy had wrapped her in silver foil. We must have looked a sight! The police pulled up but no *pompiers*. I had to answer lots of questions, James helped a lot with the translating (very handy having a sensible fluent French speaking nine-year-old in situations like these), he was brilliant. I tried phoning my Dad's mobile again and again but there was no response. The English lady asked, "Was there anyone else in the car with him?"

"Only my mum who doesn't have a mobile and my brother and I don't have his mobile number".

"Oh, and there's Ryan" piped up James. Of course, why hadn't I thought of that! Ryan was travelling with them; he had his mobile and we were always messaging each other. I called him and he answered immediately. I still had no idea where I was or where she was going to be taken but I told them to stop wherever they were and start heading back.

The *pompiers* finally arrived and there were sighs of relief all round. They tried lifting her– it wasn't easy, and she cracked a joke as they struggled to hoist her, rather ungainly, onto the stretcher. That was a good sign, I thought to myself, at least she hadn't lost her sense of humour.

I asked where they were going to take her. "Hospital Charm" they replied and pointed back towards where we came from. The policeman started to explain I needed to get off at the next exit, go back through the *péage* (toll) and towards the previous exit. All I could think was "Oh my god, what if I can't find it?" I think my panicked "rabbit in the headlights" look did the trick though, and the policeman then told me not to worry, on second thoughts it was best just to follow the ambulance through the emergency exits. Phew, that was a relief. I phoned Ryan to tell him where we were going. They tried looking it up on the sat nav but couldn't find it – great!

As the *pompiers* were getting ready to leave, I thanked the kind lady for helping us and apologised for delaying their journey. Off we set again, but this time we had a police escort! It was quite a long journey to the hospital and one I won't forget in a hurry. Firstly, we followed the ambulance through the locked emergency exit on the motorway.

"Are you sure we're allowed through here", said James who (like his mum) always worries about doing the right thing.

"I don't know, but I'm going anyway!" I told him. I was way past caring.

After travelling fast through country lanes, we came across some road works with a red light, on went the sirens and I followed the *pompiers* through. Further on, we went through a red light on a railway track – that was a bit scary, but there was no way I was letting that vehicle out of my sight, so over I went nervously checking there was no train looming. Then, I had a bit of a hairy time on a roundabout – the cars gave way to the ambulance but didn't see why they should give way to me, I was having none of it and boldly stuck my foot down. The kids thought it was great fun! Finally, we reached the hospital and the *pompiers* gestured to the car park where I needed to park. It was just as well, otherwise I'm sure I would have followed them straight into the emergency area.

In the hospital, I went to the reception desk and had to answer lots of questions (in French of course) about my cousin.

Date of birth? "I think it's in May and she's 50 something", Place of birth? "Somewhere in Buckinghamshire, England", Home address? "Somewhere in Brittany". I hadn't realised I knew so little about my cousin.

Whilst trying to answer these questions the little ones were running up and down the hospital waiting room screaming and shouting. I asked her to write down exactly where we were, and I phoned Ryan and waited while they punched the address into the sat nav ... they were about forty-five minutes away. "Forty-five minutes? Oh no!" I looked at the children, over excited, over tired and bored – good combination. I took them over to a vending machine and tried to get a bar of chocolate. It swallowed my euro and gave me nothing. So, what do I do? Cry! Tears poured down my face as I suddenly felt totally overwhelmed by the whole situation. I wanted it all to go away and leave me alone. Then, Luc looked up at me and started to giggle "It doesn't matter that much Mummy". I smiled through my tears – he was right of course.

I decided the best course of action was to take them back to the car. I couldn't stand the disapproving looks of the people in the waiting room sat with their obedient children. We sat in the car park and I gave them their packed lunch. There I was mechanically munching on a cheese and pickle roll, considering all the scenarios, tears silently streaming down my face, while the kids were squabbling in the back.

Eventually, the camper van arrived and what a relief – help at last. After giving everyone an update on what had happened, I went back into the hospital to find out what was going on. "She's still being assessed, come back in half an hour", was the response.

After a couple of hours of this, I took Ryan with me to see if he could help me understand what was going on. This time they told me I could see her, but only one person was allowed in. I left Ryan at the desk and followed them to her room. There she was, sitting up in bed smiling, legs astride and a catheter fitted. I was relieved Ryan hadn't come with me; he wouldn't have known where to look!

"They've taken four litres of wee from me and I feel so much better" she proudly announced. It seems there had been a problem with the operation she'd had earlier in the year and she hadn't been able to "go" properly for months. They were going to keep her in overnight for observation. We went back to the campervan to discuss what was best to do. We were still about six or seven hours from their home and it was about seven in the evening now. It was decided that Mum and Dad and my brother Tony would take the two youngest children and continue onto Brittany. Ryan, James and I would find a hotel for the night and take Ginny home the following morning. I was very relieved and looking forward to collapsing in a nice comfy bed after the trauma of the day. We had just pulled up at a hotel and were about to check in when my mobile rang. It was Ginny, they had discharged her after all on the promise that she must go straight to her local hospital first thing the next morning. I wasn't really feeling up to a seven-hour drive after the trauma of the day but didn't have much choice.

On the journey back to Brittany Ginny was so much brighter, she was joking about her catheter – they'd removed the bag and just left her with a pipe. "I can wee outside like a French man now", James thought this was hilarious! Later when we were discussing the day's events Ginny commented "You were so calm Nikki", I smiled,

"I didn't feel calm", was my modest reply. Then James chipped in from the back "She cried three times!" – thanks James!

A week later and after a small, successful operation Ginny informed me she was "weeing like a good un", which is preferable to weeing like a man (I think).

Driving in France

When we first moved, we thought long and hard about the best form of transport. We didn't relish the thought of buying a car in France, as we had no idea where to start. We wanted something practical, big enough to transport a family of six and three dogs; a vehicle suitable for both driving in the mountains and big enough to go away on short trips. Eventually we found our ideal vehicle and it was called a Mazda Bongo Friendee. No... I'm not joking, it really was! It was a 4 x 4, eight-seater people carrier with a pop-up roof, handy for overnight stops. The fact that you've probably never heard of it is because it was a Japanese import and that proved to be the biggest problem for us.

Re-registering a car in France is fairly straightforward as long as you have the right paperwork. The French do love their paperwork. Amongst other things, you need a certificate of conformity, which is not too difficult to get on a newish car manufactured in Britain, however getting one on a Japanese import is difficult. That was the first problem, the second was that the Bongo had a sliding door to get into the back and because it was a right-hand drive vehicle, it was on the wrong side for a country that drives on the right. We were told that we'd have to get the door moved to the opposite side before we could get approval. I'm not sure if this is true, but we decided it was too much hassle, so we sold our beloved Bongo Friendee back in the UK and bought a French registered car.

Second-hand cars are much more expensive in France, which is something you just have to accept or else go through the process of registering a UK car. Your UK car, whilst costing you less in the first place, will put you at a disadvantage when driving (especially when you get stuck behind a tractor and can't see around it) and will be difficult to sell, except to other Brits in France.

Buying and selling a car is a simple enough process, again, as long as you have all the right paperwork. The seller has to download some forms from the Internet that have to be filled in and signed (in triplicate). In the early days, one copy was sent off by the seller and the buyer took the other two to the *prefecture* where they issued the new *carte grise* (registration document). Nowadays, it is even easier as it can all be done on the Internet, although getting an account can be tricky if you don't have the right documentation...

Cars over four years old have to have a *contrôle technique* or *CT* which is the equivalent to an MOT in the UK. The *CT* is due every two years and you must display the sticker on your windscreen that shows when the next *CT* is due. When you sell a car, the *CT* must be less than six months old, even if it's not due yet. A *CT* currently costs around 75euros (2020).

There's no road tax as such in France, which is a bonus, but there are a lot of *péage* (toll roads) and they can be quite expensive. There is most often an alternative though, so you can take the slower route and avoid the toll - it depends how quickly you need to get to your destination. It's good to have a choice.

Caravans and twin axle trailers need to have their own *carte grise*, so do consider this if you're thinking of bringing one over from the UK to live here permanently. The older they are, the more difficult it will be to register them. If you don't have a certificate of conformity, you'll have to take them to a testing centre to get them physically checked. This will cost of course, but they'll tell you what changes need to be made, if any. We had to do this with a 4 x 4 Mitsubishi Pajero, which was another Japanese import. We did manage to get it registered in the end, but it took us more than eighteen months.

The insurance certificate is issued on green paper and is known as the *carte verte*. It has a little tear off square at the bottom of the certificate that should be displayed on the windscreen. It's obligatory in France to carry your *carte gris* and *carte vert* in your car at all times as well as your driving licence. If you are stopped and you don't have them, you may be fined. You also have to carry a high vis vest and a warning triangle. There was talk of having to carry a breathalyser kit too, but I don't think that's been enforced because they couldn't get enough supplies for everyone. I just see it as another way for them to make money anyway.

Insurance is a bit different to the UK. All insurance policies (not just car insurance) can only be cancelled on the anniversary of when you took out the insurance and this must be done in writing at least two months before the renewal date by registered post. If you don't, and miss by even one day (as we have personal experience of doing), the cancellation request will be invalid, and you will be stuck with the same insurance policy another year. It is a real pain! That is the downside, but there are upsides as we've found that generally car insurance is cheaper here and simpler in lots of ways as you insure the car rather than the driver. It makes it easier to lend your car to visitors, as long as the person has a valid driving licence, they are covered to drive the car.

We bought a second-hand car for Matthew for his seventeenth birthday. It was cheap (I think we paid about 300€) because it was a right-hand drive car registered in France. He was living in the UK, so we thought he could take it back and re-register it in England when he'd passed his test. Unfortunately, this never happened. The first summer holiday after we had bought it, he came home bringing his friend Charlie to stay. Charlie had already passed his driving test and they took the car out with him as the driver. He was driving along a winding country road and as he took the corner, a baguette fell off the back seat. Taking his eyes momentarily off the road, Charlie turned back to see what had fallen and then crashed into a little stone wall on the edge of the road. The car was a write-off, but luckily the boys weren't seriously hurt. They were very shaken up but thankfully only suffered a bit of whiplash and a few cuts. If anything, it was a good thing as it made Matthew more cautious on the road as he knows how easily accidents can happen.

The insurance claim was very straightforward and although we had to pay an excess of 1000€ for the young driver, we got more than we had paid for the car as they assessed it at the price of the left hand drive equivalent, so we didn't really lose anything.

Parking is a bugbear of mine, it's so infuriating! There are some in France who will park anywhere! At the supermarket, they'll park right outside the entrance, blocking all the traffic and without a thought for other drivers, even when the car park is virtually empty. They'll double park, park on yellow lines, park in front of garages. It's as if the rules are there to be broken. I've never seen a traffic warden and rarely a car clamp, so that's probably why.

Parking is cheap in rural areas and more often than not free, but you do have to watch the signs in the car parks as certain times are prohibited. Unfortunately, Matthew discovered this the hard way one fateful weekend. During his friend Charlie's visit (before he wrote off the car), they decided to go on a night out in Toulouse and who could blame them, there's not a lot happening for teenagers in our area. When they arrived in Toulouse, which is just over an hour's drive from us, they parked in a car park which appeared to be free. They found a hotel for the night and went in search of some night life. Apparently, they found it, had a great evening and went back to the hotel to sleep it off. The following morning, they returned to where they had left the car and as they approached their hearts sank. The car park was now a full, busy and bustling market! The car was nowhere to be seen. After a panicked time of asking stall holders where the car could be, they spent the day going back and forth between police stations and the car pound. Finally, after paying a hefty fine, they got the car back and drove rather dejectedly home, only to write it off in the accident mentioned above a few days later! Sometimes life deals some tough cards...

Learning to drive is an expensive business. You can't just buy L plates, get a provisional licence and start driving on the road with a qualified driver, as you can in the UK. You either have to have lessons with a driving instructor or you opt for a system of accompanied driving, where a nominated, competent driver can drive with you. Although you can start to learn as accompanied driver at sixteen, you can't take your test until you are eighteen. It's much more regulated than it is in the UK, which is quite mystifying as many French drivers are appalling! I don't know what they teach them here at driving school, but it would appear that they're taught to drive from A to B as fast as possible, driving so close to the car in front that they can see the hairs on the back of the driver's neck. It would seem, for some drivers in France, overtaking is best done on corners and approaching the brow of a hill. I have found that drivers are generally more polite in the UK and the difference is noticeable when you start driving in France. The French are lovely, kind, polite people, but once behind a wheel, many turn into impatient monsters.

Our middle son James decided to go for a *permis* A motorbike licence when he turned sixteen to learn to drive a 125cc motorbike. I understood why - we live in the middle of nowhere and it's at least thirty minutes' drive to any of his friends (so a one-hour round trip for me to drop him off). I've never really moaned about being a taxi-driver for the children, after all we decided to live in a rural area, and it was always going to be more difficult as the children got older. However, James decided he'd rather have the freedom to go where he pleases and not have to rely on me. You can drive a 50cc scooter at fourteen in France and many 14-year-olds do, Ryan did. However, a 50cc bike is not really substantial enough to drive too far and I never liked him to go too far on it.

The *permis* A is very expensive - it cost around 1000 euros which includes the theory lessons and the theory test (which is the same as for driving a car), twenty hours of bike lessons and two practical tests. All in all, it took him about five months to get his licence, but he's glad he did. I know he's a safe driver, but I can't help worrying about him as there are some scary drivers on the road. However, you can't live your life like that, and he has had so much more freedom since he's had his bike. It's also been one less child for me to taxi around.

Apart from some challenging drivers, driving in France is generally an enjoyable experience. The motorways are excellent, the motorway services are good, and they have lots of *aires,* which are stopping places with good facilities. The roads are less congested in our area and driving can be a very pleasant experience. Inevitably, there are a few other things that make driving less pleasurable at times such as tractors with heavy loads of hay (living in an agricultural area that's only to be expected, I suppose), narrow roads with excessively deep ditches, lots of cyclists (this is *Tour de France* country) and poor signage. Signs and roadworks are lacking in places and not only in the country. But, the most annoying thing is when you come across roadworks where a diversion is in place. There will often be a sign in place to guide you towards an alternative route and then the signs will disappear almost immediately. I've come across this many times – it seems as though whoever put out the signs really doesn't care which route you take as long as you don't take this one! The first time I experienced this was on the way back from a trip to the airport after picking up another friend of Matthew's who'd come to stay. We'd probably only been here about a year, so I wasn't too familiar with the roads. We came across some roadworks and I was pointed in another direction. After a short while, the signs completely disappeared, and I had no idea where I was. I was navigating through lots of little country lanes weaving this way and that in the pitch black. It took me an extra hour to get home that night – I was not impressed.

Another regular sight here is the *fauchage* – the team of council workers who are responsible for cutting the hedgerows and butchering (sorry did I say butchering, I meant pruning) the trees. Sometimes you'll come around a corner and suddenly there's a set of temporary traffic lights without warning, (that's if you get any warning at all). Other times it will be a man with a lollipop sign with red or green on either side. He'll stand there for ages with it showing red, avoiding eye contact before he suddenly realises there are no cars coming, so he'll call his lollipop mate at the other end of the road to see if it's safe to turn it to green. Or, more usually you might spy a red flag tied to a signpost at the edge of the road (often just after or on a blind corner) and a few feet on you'll find the *fauchage* blocking the road – it really is very dangerous.

Many locals have a blatant disrespect for roadwork signs (where there are any). It is not uncommon for them to just ignore a no entry sign and take the road anyway. Having got lost several times following a diversion sign I can understand why. We had to block off the road that passes in front of our house for a few days when the scaffolding was up to render the front. We got all the permissions and were given the appropriate signs by the local council, but the local hunt just totally ignored the signs and ploughed their way through regardless. As we stood there staring at them in disbelief, they just boldly carried on as if this was an everyday occurrence (well it probably was for them). Another example was when the school road was blocked off for a week when they were repairing it. Rather than take an extra two minutes and go around the block, everyone just ignored the no entry signs and drove over the roadworks to get into the school. Something you just wouldn't see in the UK. It took us some courage, but we followed suit in the end, nobody seemed to care and if you can't beat them, join them!

Safety standards in rural areas in my experience are generally much lower. There are all sorts of red tape, paperwork and hoops to jump through to get permission to do anything, but once you've got the permission it seems anything goes. I've seen several supermarkets get revamped since living here and it amazes me how they keep the shops open whilst the building work is going on. Recently a shop in a local town had half the car park up with diggers driving around. There were no signs to show where you were supposed to park and none of the building work was cordoned off. It seemed you just had to find a piece of tarmac that hadn't been dug up, leave your car in the hope it didn't get demolished whilst shopping, climb over the uneven dug up car park, duck through the scaffolding and hope nothing fell on your unprotected head. Once you'd navigated those hazards you stepped into the half-demolished shop to buy your groceries, like this was perfectly normal and safe. Incredible!

Although the road and building works are generally badly signposted and safety policies leave a little to be desired, there are lots of things that the French do get right and are ahead of the UK in. One example of this is a system called *covoiturage* (car sharing). There is a website now called www.blablacar.fr where drivers travelling from city to city with empty seats in the car can advertise and offer places at a cheap rate to other travellers. It works out cheaper than travelling by train and is an economic use of the car. It's a bit like eBay in that users of the service can rate the drivers and the passengers to make it safer. Drivers and passengers have to register their details and create an account. My older boys used it a lot to travel around to other cities. You book in advance online and make contact with the driver to arrange a suitable pick up point from somewhere like a motorway exit or train station. We advertised spaces once on blablacar when we travelled from home to Nice and back. It paid for the journey and we met some very interesting people which made the time pass quicker. It's a win win situation.

People sometimes ask how I cope with driving on the other side of the road. It's really not that difficult. Yes, it feels a bit strange to start with, but you soon get used to it. It's more difficult of course if you have a right-hand drive car because (as I said above) you can't see around the tractors and lorries, but it's not impossible. Also, the gear stick and handbrake are on the other side in a left-hand drive car. Again, it feels a bit strange to start with, but you quickly get used to it – it's like getting used to an automatic after using a manual and vice versa. I used to be a bit apprehensive about driving different vehicles, but since moving here I've driven left hand and right-hand drive, manual and automatic, 4 x 4's, a seven-seater Pontiac, various vans and a dumper truck! I've driven a van with a trailer on the back down to Spain and I've driven a clapped-out campervan on a 12-hour journey from the UK on my own with a baby on board.

There seem to be more spot checks by police here than in the UK. In twenty years of driving in England I had never been stopped, but Gary and I have been stopped many times since moving to France. Once I was driving home after doing my taxi driving duties for Ryan who was seventeen at the time when I was confronted by a policeman who beckoned me to pull over. My heart sank. I immediately felt guilty – why is it that even the sight of a policeman can make you feel guilty when you've done nothing wrong? It was rather fortunate really because just the day before I'd noticed that the *carte verte* displayed on the windscreen of my car had expired by two weeks. This is usually sent a month or so in advance, so I realised I must have missed the letter somehow. It had been a busy few months (or should I say years) and I'd got a bit behind with the paperwork. That morning I persuaded Ryan that if he wanted that lift to town in the afternoon the deal was, he watched the little ones while I do a bit of paperwork. I set to work going through the papers on my desk and right at the bottom was an unopened envelope from our insurance company *et voila* – the missing green insurance paper I was looking for. So, I popped the appropriate piece into the plastic wallet on my dashboard and made lunch.

I know it's not a spectacular miracle as miracles go, but I was so relieved that I'd found it just in time, when literally hours later I was pulled over for the first time in years. I'm not sure what the penalty would have been for not having the appropriate insurance displayed, but I'm sure they would have given me more of a hard time and if nothing else I would have had to go to the police station later to produce the document.

As it was, he pointed to my youngest in a car seat in the back and said "*ceinture?*" (seat belt), so I leaned over and showed him the seat belt it was just hidden by a tee shirt. He then proceeded to study the lights and tyres (which we'd happened to have replaced only the week before as they were dangerously low). He studied the insurance disc (phew) and the *CT*... all OK. Checked the back brakes – all fine. Then he asked if I had my driving licence on me. Yes, I did and I knew exactly where it was as I had looked at it earlier that day while in "paperwork" mode. I handed it over and the policeman studied it and asked if I was Ukrainian and pointed to the UK on the licence. Really?

"*Non, Anglaise*". I explained, UK stands for United Kingdom – *Royaume-Uni*! Surely, he'd seen a British licence before? I didn't say that out loud of course. I was about to get my passport out to prove it, but he took my word for it and allowed me on my way without another word. He was probably too embarrassed to say anything else. This was when I still had a British licence...

To change or not to change your driving licence

When we moved to France from the UK there was no hint of Brexit, the UK was in the EU and UK licences were acceptable in France, there was no need to change unless stopped by the gendarmes/police for a driving offence and given points (they can't put them on a UK licence). However, since Brexit has reared its ugly head, these rules may no longer apply, and British citizens are being advised to exchange their licences. You will have to exchange your driving licence anyway when your UK photocard expires. Many people don't realise that the UK card licences are only valid for a maximum of ten years and I was one of them.

Unfortunately for me, I discovered it too late as my licence had already expired by six months. Now, I know many British in France (prior to the referendum) renewed their UK licences to a UK address and I can understand why. Anyone who's lived here a while and experienced the joys of French bureaucracy will do anything to avoid it. However, I live here permanently, we're not planning on going back to the UK, we don't have a house in the UK and my parents were living here too at the time, so we couldn't use their address. There was no getting away from it (I felt), I just had to give up my UK licence and trade it in for French one.

My first stop was the *sous préfecture* in our local town of Saint-Gaudens. Each department in France has a *préfecture* in the department capital which is the main administrative centre for things like visas, car registrations and driving licences. Each department has several *sous-préfectures* in major towns which are sub-offices of the main *préfecture* and can perform most of the functions of the main *préfecture* locally. Our main *préfecture* is in Toulouse and is about one and a half hours from our home (taking into account traffic and parking in a big city) and our *sous préfecture* is in Saint-Gaudens just twenty minutes away, so I obviously opted for this first. When I asked about how to exchange my licence, they told me there was no need to change my UK licence. Yes, I know, but I pointed out that the date had expired. I was met with a puzzled look. Surely, I'm not the first person to have a licence expire in this area? She scuttled off and came back with some papers - fill these in and take them to the *préfecture* in Toulouse. Really? Can't I do it here? Can't I send them? No, it has to be Toulouse and I have to go in person. So, I sighed, filed the papers in the depths of my bag, and there they would stay until I could muster up the time and strength to battle the administrative heart of the Haute Garonne department. I know it sounds a bit melodramatic, but it really is that bad, trust me I've been through it too many times.

Several months later (June 2013) I was planning a trip to England to see Matthew graduate with a Masters in Chemistry from Bristol University. The options were either to fly and hire a car or drive – either way the fact that my driving licence had expired raised its ugly head and there was no putting it off any longer, I HAD to change my licence. I dug out the dog-eared papers from the depths of my bag and trawled the expat forums to see what else I might need and how long it might take. I asked the question on one of the Facebook groups I belong to and I could not believe how different the experiences were. Some had no trouble at all, and it was done on the spot, some had to wait a couple of weeks and for others it took months... I discovered that I needed a certificate from DVLA to confirm that whilst my photocard had expired, my licence was still in fact valid until 2036. I rang the DVLA and within five minutes the certificate was faxed to me. Take note all you French administrators, it was that simple - oh how I miss that!

So, I set off to the *préfecture* in Toulouse with all I needed and more (just in case). It wasn't easy for me to get time off work at the time. We had a garden centre to run which I was manning single-handedly, so I had to close the business for the day and not only annoy our customers, but also lose business. The *préfecture* is a massive building full of people waiting and waiting and waiting. I had a quick look round, found where I needed to queue and took a ticket from the machine, which very kindly informed me that there were 45 people ahead of me, great!

One and a half hours later and my number came up at last! I handed over all the paperwork to the woman behind the counter. She took it all and asked me to wait. Another hour passed and a man called my name and asked for my birth and marriage certificates. I had my birth certificate, but unfortunately not my marriage certificate. Luckily, he decided that wasn't necessary after all and he disappeared back into the office clutching my file. Another thirty minutes passed, and he reappeared with a letter. As my licence had expired, he informed me, I needed to have a medical! Why? I asked. It's the photo that's expired not my licence. Had I renewed it six months earlier I wouldn't have needed a medical, so why now? It made no sense. But there was no reasoning with him. Rules are rules and these are this particular *préfecture*'s rules. However, he did add that the file was complete, all I needed was the medical certificate which would be sent back directly to them with no need for me to come back. They would then send me a letter to say my new licence was ready and then I would have to go back to Toulouse in person to collect it and surrender my UK licence. If I didn't get the medical, my licence would no longer be valid in France. No choice then. I came away more than a little frustrated. I knew there was no way I'd get my new licence before my trip to England which was only two weeks away.

The *préfecture* had given me a list of approved doctors for the medical and I was relieved to find one in Saint-Gaudens. I made an early morning appointment for the following week; I didn't think it would take long, so I expected to be back in time to open the garden centre by 10am. I arrived in good time and gave the letter from the *préfecture* to the receptionist. She looked at it blankly, like she'd never come across this before. She fumbled through some files then spoke to the doctor. He scratched his head and asked if I could come back another day. "No" I firmly replied. My look of horror did the trick. She rang the *sous-préfecture*, fumbled through some more files then produced a pink form. I went into the doctor who checked my blood pressure, listened to my chest, asked if I had any problems and checked my eyesight. It took less than five minutes and he charged me 35 euros (which is not refunded with my *carte vitale*). Back at the receptionist desk, she photocopied everything three times and handed the originals to me and told me to take it to the *préfecture* in Toulouse. My heart sank, "No, it's you who send it directly to the *préfecture*", I said. I was not taking another day off work to go Toulouse just to hand in some papers. I pointed to the letter where it clearly stated that the doctor should forward the papers to the préfecture. The receptionist scowled and phoned the *sous-préfecture* in Saint-Gaudens. No, they confirmed I would have to take the forms to Toulouse. I got really angry now, I'd already wasted more time than I could afford. There was no way I was going to waste another full day round trip to Toulouse and 30 euros in petrol and parking (not to mention the money lost from closing the shop). I pointed again to the letter, "this is from the *PREFECTURE* and they say YOU send it", I stressed in my best and most heated French. The receptionist shrugged and refused to take the papers. I could see I was not going to win. I would have sent them myself, but I knew what sticklers they were for things to be done correctly and I didn't want my file to get mysteriously lost or something. I drove across town to the *sous-préfecture*. Waited an hour before explaining the situation to the woman behind the counter. She read the letter from the *préfecture*: "The doctor should send these papers", at last, someone with a brain. "Yes, I know I tried to tell her that, but she wouldn't listen". She told me not to worry, she'd take the papers and give them to the lady that deals with licences and she'd send them to Toulouse. She took my number in case there were any problems.

That was at the end of June. July came and Matthew's graduation was drawing near and I was desperate to go. I decided to drive as I couldn't hire a car with an expired licence and at least if I got stopped, I had all the paperwork to prove I was in the process of changing my licence. It was an expensive trip and money was very tight, so I decided the only way I could do it was to take the van and get the trip paid for by collecting and delivering a few things for friends. Seemed like a good idea at the time. My trip started with a detour to Bordeaux to pick up an emergency passport for James (whose passport unfortunately hadn't arrived in time). Then onto Brittany to pick up my cousin who was going to visit her parents in England. Then a stop off in Kent to spend a few days with family, then a couple of days in Bristol to see Matthew receive his Masters in Chemistry (so proud). Day eight of my trip was the busiest - I delivered some furniture to a friend in Devon, picked up a load for another friend in Poole (to be delivered to France), picked up some stock for Gary in Eastleigh, then onto High Wycombe (through rush hour traffic) to pick up my cousin. Overnight stop with my aunt and uncle, then back to Dover, dropped my cousin back off in Brittany (a journey that took ten hours instead of six because the van kept losing power uphill.) Do you know how many hills there are on the way from Calais to Brittany? Too many!! Luckily it was nothing serious, just a pipe had fallen off from somewhere it shouldn't have (at least that's what I think the mechanic said) and finally I drove the ten hours back home. Four thousand kms and a couple of minor breakdowns later (the van and me that is) and got home safe and sound. Radiohead's song "You do it to yourself" springs to mind!

August was drawing to a close and I was beginning to wonder if my application for a driving licence was still sitting in a tray in Saint-Gaudens *sous-préfecture*, when a letter arrived to say that my licence was ready and I had to come in person on Wednesday 29th August between 9-12.15 with my old licence. At last! It had taken over nine weeks. Nine weeks to get a very amateur looking pink piece of thin card with my photo stuck on it! The worse thing was, after waiting all that time for this poor excuse of a licence, I was informed that I'll have to change it again next year as two weeks later they were changing over to the new card licences like the UK!

So, the moral of this story is, hang on to your UK licence as long as you can, but make sure you sort out a new one before it expires! After the hassle we had changing my licence we decided to renew Gary's in the UK, I sometimes wish I had done that too. I've since found other difficulties with having a French licence, such as arranging temporary car insurance for helping to drive a friends UK car from the UK to France. However, when I hire a car in the UK with my French licence I don't have to send off for the new checks from the DVLA, and when I get stopped in France I no longer have the "you must change your licence lecture" from the gendarmes, so there are advantages.

What about the weather?

Ask any Brit why they moved from the UK and one of the most common answers will be a topic most British people obsess about - the weather. So, has the weather in France lived up to our expectations?

Generally speaking, here in the Southwestern corner of France we enjoy long hot summers, but the winters, although short, are much colder than we had anticipated. We also get a fair amount of rain, so the countryside is much greener here than it is on the other side of the mountains in Spain. We seem to get extremes of weather, for example it doesn't hail often, but when it does the hailstones are huge; it's generally not that windy, but when the wind does blow it will knock you off your feet and I've witnessed some far more spectacular storms than I've ever experienced in the UK.

The temperature in autumn is usually very pleasant. We arrived in France at the end of September 2004 and our first month here was very hot. We were all in T-shirts and shorts and yet we couldn't understand why all the locals were in jumpers. We came to the conclusion that they must have acclimatised to the weather, something we never thought we would, but a year or so later and we found that we were the ones in jumpers and you can spot the tourists a mile off wandering around in shorts and flip-flops!

October that first year saw daytime temperatures approaching 30°C at times, it felt so great to leave the dreary cold and windy weather behind us. However, we were being lulled into a false sense of security. November came and it was as if someone had flipped a switch and winter arrived overnight. The wind came howling through the broken windows and cracks and suddenly we realised the urgency of making our home warm. We had no idea it would get that cold – night-time temperatures plummeted to -10°C whereas during the day it would sometimes still get up to 20°C. We had asked the locals when we arrived about the chances of snow and were reliably informed that it very rarely snows here. But, of course, that year was the exception and we awoke one morning to see our lake and canal covered with frost and the land a foot deep in snow. It arrived very unexpectedly, and we didn't have time to prepare – we just had to attempt to deal with it.

We were shown how to use the central heating system, a heat exchange system, when we bought the house. It takes the calories from the air and turns them into heat – excellent we thought. I'm not sure if it had been fitted incorrectly or if it was just old, but it only ever seemed to make the radiators lukewarm and when it snowed the system froze up completely inside and we had to abandon it. We had a big fireplace in the sitting room, so we swept out the chimney and started to use that. It looked lovely, but you could only feel the heat if you stood directly in front of it. Most of the heat generated swooped up the chimney. We soon discovered that chimney building was not a forte in these parts! So, we wore coats and scarves indoors during the day and at night-time, we huddled under duvet covers in front of the TV. In fact, when it was really cold, we went to bed fully clothed – it was like camping indoors and was quite miserable! Having now spent many winters here we've found them generally short but often very cold. We light the fires from late November/early December - March/April.

Come February we've always had enough of winter and Gary starts trawling the Internet in search of hotter countries to live in. I know the winters are much shorter than in the UK, but they can be very harsh and poor Gary has to work out in them. Luckily, the weather usually starts warming up between the middle of March and the middle of April when we stop having to light our wood fires and we can put our coats away until November and all thoughts of moving to warmer climes are forgotten. Spring is often warm but can be quite wet too, but the wet weather is interspersed with beautiful sunny days and picnics and barbecues often start around May. Spring is also the time when we are most likely to get hail and often very large hailstones sometimes the size of golf balls. They've been known to dent cars, bruise people and have ruined our stock of plants on more than one occasion. We've had several severe hail storms over the past few years and several of our friends and neighbours have had to have their entire roofs re-laid - luckily we haven't lost our roof (so far), but we have had damage to the bodywork of our car and van and several windscreens broken. There is always a sense of panic when the sky turns black in the spring and early summer and the threat of hail is near.

Summer is usually long and hot. It's often hot in May and June but can be quite changeable. We are usually guaranteed hot weather in July and August with temperatures averaging around 28-30°C. The weather seems to build up here getting hotter and hotter and then we'll have a massive storm (often overnight) which will clear the air and reduce the heat to a more comfortable temperature. The storms are very localised. and often quite spectacular with lots of forked and sheet lightning. As we are close to the Pyrenees, often in the summer we can see fantastic electrical storms in the mountains. We can see hours of flashing lights, but don't hear the thunder as they are too far away. They are spectacular to watch, but not so great to drive through. On our way on holiday to Spain across the Pyrenees a few years back we drove through one of those spectacular storms in the early hours of the morning. It was terrifying, I'm only glad I wasn't driving!

The evenings in the summer (when it's not storming) are often warm and comfortable enough to sit outside and we enjoy many an evening barbecuing followed by a game of cards, a few glasses of wine and often round off the evening studying the stars in the crystal clear night skies. Generally, the weather is not as windy as it is on the Kent Coast, however it is so changeable. It can be dead still one minute and then the wind can whip up out of nowhere. In January 2009 we experienced our first hurricane in France. Luckily, it had been forecast (unlike the one in the UK in 1987), obviously Michel Poisson knows his stuff here! We knew there was a hurricane on its way and due to hit us in the early hours of the morning. I'd seen a message from one of my friends on Facebook and then I looked it up on *Météo-France*. We went around the house closing all the shutters – no mean feat on a building with over forty windows!

Sure enough, in the early hours of the morning we were awoken by the howling wind. The shutterless windows in our bedroom were rattling, the house was shaking and all we could do was wait until morning to assess the damage. Daylight came and the hurricane continued. We stood at the windows of our sitting room watching the debris flying past. "Oh my god, I think that poplar's going to go" and before Gary had finished the sentence the enormous tree came crashing down across the road and onto the electricity cable knocking out ours and everyone else's power in the area.

"I'll have to move it."

"You can't go out in that, it's too dangerous", I reasoned

"I've got to try, no one can get past. What if there's an emergency?"

There was no stopping him. Off he ventured, chainsaw in hand as I looked on nervously from the window above. Despite the strength of the wind and the branches flying around he managed to cut up the main stem crossing the lane and drag it to the side of the road.

We lost several trees and were without electricity for some time. The first night was the worst. We have such a large sitting room it was difficult to get enough light from any candles to see anything. We had tea lights all over the room, but it was still largely dark. Ryan and James had to do their homework by candlelight and it was really difficult to even see where our youngest was. Going up to bed was a challenge too and leaving tea lights shining in the children's bedrooms frightened me to death. After three days of no electricity, *EDF (Electricité de France*, the main electric supplier in France) came and temporarily fixed the line. Well, you can imagine, suddenly all the washing machines, heating, tumble dryers, dishwashers, etc., went on. Later that day we heard a big buzzing sound and the computer and the lights flashed off and on. This happened a couple of times and then I could hear some large cracks and buzzing coming from outside. I looked out of the window only to see the box that EDF had fixed was on fire and had massive sparks showering down from it like a Catherine wheel. It was quite spectacular, and I managed to get some footage of it on my camera which you can see on YouTube. I rushed downstairs

152

and switched off the mains and we were another four days without electricity until EDF finally came out and fixed it properly.

Power cuts are far more frequent here than they are in the UK. It's not only common to lose electricity in a storm, but often it's for no apparent reason. In fact, whilst writing this chapter the electricity just went off with no warning. Extremely frustrating if you haven't saved your work recently! It was out for about half an hour then came back on again. One New Year's Eve we had a big party (as we often do) and this time we had a live band playing. Unfortunately, about thirty minutes before the band were due to play the electricity went out. At first, we thought it had tripped and we fumbled around in the dark trying to find the trip switches. However, after a while we discovered that everyone else's lights had gone out too. We had a house full of about sixty people, food, tables, etc., and no lights! Luckily, I managed to find plenty of tea lights in a cupboard downstairs – a small miracle because I wasn't sure where I had put them. I spent the next hour lighting candles and spreading them in a line leading to the loo, down the two sets of stairs, on all the tables and anywhere I could. I was in a panic – how were the band going to play, what a disaster. But everyone seemed quite happy sitting and chatting and the band began playing acoustically. Everyone said it added to the atmosphere and seemed to enjoy the novelty of it. It was a great relief when the lights came back on about 11.30pm, the band plugged in and we managed to get some dancing in and "see" in the New Year.

Speaking the lingo

Not many people speak English here and so it is essential to speak at least some French. It's amazing how you can get by with only a little French. However, you do miss out on a large chunk of French life if you don't master the language, so it really is worth making the effort.

When we first moved to France, our French was quite basic. I had just scraped through my O level French. I really wish I'd tried a bit harder at school, but at the time I remember thinking I'd never use it again, so I didn't see the point. Little did I know that I would end up living in France later in life, which might well have given me the incentive I needed. I only chose to take French at school because the alternative option was geography and I really didn't like that at all. I had some basics in French (largely due to the fact that I had disliked the geography teacher more than the French) but it had been over twenty years since I had used it, so I was very rusty. It's amazing how it starts seeping back though and gradually I started recalling things I didn't even know I knew in the first place. I had intended taking lessons, but being pregnant on arrival, having a massive building to renovate, settling our kids into school and trying to get to grips with the system and general living, I really didn't have the time to fit French lessons in too. I'm fairly proficient now. I'm not as fluent as I would like to be, but I can understand virtually all that is said to me, can hold a conversation, answer the telephone (which is probably the hardest thing) and have sufficient French to communicate both verbally and in writing to manage the day to day running of our businesses. I no longer have to sit there for ten minutes working out what to say on the phone before I make a call or have a meeting, I can usually ask straight off for the information I need. And how have I got to this stage? Well I found by talking to neighbours, doctors, gynaecologists, teachers, etc., my French has gradually improved. I bought a book on medical terms, which was very useful in the early days and I listened to tapes when I could. I took a few lessons, but not as many as I'd like as it is difficult to find the time (and financial constraints). In the early days I listened to the Michel Thomas CDs which really helped me to brush up on my French. Although basic, they are great for getting started and building confidence to create sentences and communicate. I find listening to the French radio helps too. I've tried French TV, but it's just too boring. We used to have English satellite at home, however they changed the satellite settings a few years ago and we would have to have upgraded our dish to 1.2m and it still wasn't guaranteed to receive a signal. As our internet connection is good, we now watch English TV programs via the Internet, Netflix, YouTube, etc., on our smart TV or laptop. I suppose you could say we will never be fully integrated into French life until we have French TV and give up all our English habits. That may be the best thing for some people, but we're not trying to be French. We live in France; we love France and its people but we are of British descent and nothing can change that. No matter how much we try to integrate we will always be "*les Anglais*". So instead of trying to be something we're not, we live a blended life of England and France – embracing the things we like about France and holding on to some of the traditions we've grown up with. How our children will develop from here and their children will be interesting to discover. Will our grandchildren retain some of our English ways or will they be more French than English?

Gary had virtually no French at all when we arrived. He had been excluded from his French class in the first year of secondary school for not paying attention and so he had a few odd words but no grammar at all. He had some very funny encounters in the early days. Our neighbour Emile loved to chat to Gary or "Guy" (pronounced Gee) as he used to call him. Whenever Gary was outside working on something, Emile would wander up to watch him and try to chat. Emile had a very strong local accent and even our children struggled to understand him sometimes, so Gary and I didn't have much chance. But with Emile and Gary it was more instinctive. Gary often knew what Emile was saying by his gestures (and the fact that it was almost always related to whatever he was doing). One day, Gary came in after one of his long chats with Emile looking a bit confused.

"How's Emile?" I asked.

"Oh, Okay, I think. He was talking about the Mayor. He said he was a duck – I suppose he means he's a bit of an idiot."

"A duck?"

"Yes, he said he was a 'Mallard'"

"A mallard? Are you sure he didn't say he was '*malade*'?"

"Yes, that's it. He said something like "*Il est malade*""

"Oh Gary, that means he's ill! '*Malade*' means 'ill'"

"Oh dear, that would explain his puzzled look when I laughed when I thought he said he was a mallard and said "*Oui, tous les mêmes*" (Gary's way of saying, yes they are all the same these officials). Emile forgave him. I think he got quite used to us getting the wrong end of the stick and so when we made inappropriate responses, he made allowances for us as he knew we were just "*les Anglais*". Gary learnt lots of useful words from Emile like *tronçonneuse* (chainsaw), *tondeuse* (lawn mower), *débroussailleuse* (brush cutter), caillou (stone) and other very practical vocabulary. Gary was getting much better on his "working" vocabulary of tools and such like than I was. Whereas I was forging ahead with medical and pregnancy terms, such as "*Je voudrais une péridural*" ("I want an epidural"). His French grammar was progressing very slowly but over the past couple of years it has come on in leaps and bounds and that's largely due to when he had a French apprentice working with him. It forced him to speak French on a daily basis. Arthur spoke very little English when he started with us – by the end of the second year of his apprenticeship he spoke and understood a lot. They had a great understanding between them and spoke a mixture of French and English or *Franglais*. Gary now understands most of what is said to him and can respond and make himself understood, even if it's not totally grammatically correct.

There are lots of courses available to help you learn French, so there really isn't any excuse. It's also a good way to meet other people. It's true to say though that the older you are the more difficult it is.

Learning the language is a different process for the children. When we first moved here we did consider whether it might be better to try to speak French at home to help the children adapt at school, but to be honest, our French really wasn't good enough and I think it would have been more of a hindrance than a help.

It's amazing how adaptable children are and how quickly they learn to cope with switching from one language to the other. We've never made a big deal about it and neither have they. James found his own way of asking whether he should be speaking French or English when he used to ask "Mummy, do they say hello or *bonjour*?".

We're often asked how long it took for our children to be fluent. It's been slightly different for each of them. Ryan was ten when we moved here and had hardly any French. He says the first three months he hadn't got a clue what was being said to him at school, but then over the next nine months his French got stronger and stronger. By the end of the first year he had enough French to move onto the College and within eighteen months he was largely fluent.

James was two and half when we arrived in France and started at the *maternelle* at three years old with no French at all. He said nothing in class for about the first twelve months and we weren't sure if he was really learning or not, although the teachers said he understood what was being said to him. Between twelve and eighteen months after starting school he started speaking French and he started speaking full sentences. It was as though he didn't want to speak until he could be sure he would get it right.

Luc started school at two and a half. He didn't have much French as we only spoke English at home but had at least been exposed to it during the first few years of his life. He was much more confident at school and was more ready to speak in French, but it was still at least 18 months before he was speaking fluently.

None of the children like us speaking to them in French, I think although they can speak French fluently now, English is still their first language, so when at home they prefer to speak English as it's no effort for them. I bought lots of French children's books to read to them when they were little, but they wouldn't let me read to them in French. I had to translate them into English! We watch TV largely in English. We did have French TV for a while, but no one watched it. We watch most programmes and films in English, but the children watch them in French if they have friends over.

Our children all speak English with an English accent, however I know of an English family where the children speak with a French accent, but they have French TV only and speak a lot of French at home, so maybe that's why. We are told that our three youngest children speak French with a local accent and it's not possible to tell they are English. Ryan apparently has a slight accent, but people often think he's from another part of France. When he was helping another student with his English homework once, some of the other students asked why he was helping him. They didn't know he was English. Matthew has the strongest English accent of all the children, but that's because he was largely taught French whilst at school in England. He did spend his third year of his degree studying in Montpellier though, so he's really become proficient now.

We were talking at the dinner table one evening about accents and the fact that the French find it difficult to pronounce the sound 'th'. I asked James, who was nine at the time, if his teacher ever got him to speak during their English lessons to help the others know how to pronounce the words properly.

'No, the teacher tells us what to say.'

'Well at least when you repeat it, they'll hear how to say it properly.' I reasoned.

'No, I say it with the same accent as the teacher.'

I found this quite funny, well really funny actually. Sorry, but imagining him '*speeeking like zis*' in class just tickled me. When I stopped laughing, I asked 'Why on earth do you do that?'

'Because that is how you have to speak English in France.'

We explained to James that he actually spoke English with a correct English accent and that the others could learn from him. He assured me he used his normal accent after that. Ryan says he often has to say the titles of films and books to his friends with a French accent in English otherwise they don't understand him.

It's so lovely to hear the children talking away in French to each other so naturally. What a wonderful gift to be able to speak two languages effortlessly and fluently - one of the many benefits of growing up in a foreign country.

Another aspect we have had to learn to contend with is regional accents. As I mentioned previously, the accent in the Southwest of France where we live is very different to that in the north. We have difficulty understanding them even now that we are used to the accent sometimes and lots of the French have difficulty understanding us – even if we are saying the right word, which is very disconcerting at times. You can repeat the same word five times trying different accents and they still frown and scratch their heads at you. Then, when the penny drops and they realise what you're trying to say and they repeat the word, you think to yourself "Well, that was exactly what I said". I've noticed that the locals who are more used to dealing with non-native speakers understand us better than those who haven't had much exposure.

It's one thing speaking and understanding French with a French person, but it's quite another speaking French to a non-native speaker. There are lots of Dutch in this area, most of them are better at speaking English than French and so once they realise we are English, they'll start speaking with us in English. However, some prefer to speak in French and speaking French with someone whose mother tongue is different from your own is tricky as you have to get to know their accent and way of speaking French which is different to ours. One such example of this happened within our first year. Our Dutch neighbour was passing by and stopped for a chat with Gary who was working outside. He normally speaks in English to us, but often slips into French. They were discussing chickens as we had just got some new ones. The conversation went something like this:

"So, you have some chickens now Gary."

"Yes, they've just started to lay a few eggs".

"You have *un oeuf?*"

"Yes, we have *oeufs.*"

"But do you have *un oeuf?*"

"Yes, we have *un oeuf.*" Gary repeated very slowly and unsurely. He called to me to come and help as he couldn't understand why Wilhem kept asking him if he had "*un oeuf*" (an egg in French).

"Hello Nikki, I was just asking Gary if you had enough eggs because you know we have lots if you are needing some", said a very confused looking Wilhem, wondering why Gary kept repeating "eggs" in French (*oeufs*).

"Oh ENOUGH, Gary thought you were saying "*un oeuf*". That's very kind of you, but we have plenty."

I was used to helping with translating from French to English, but not translating from English to English!

Family ties

One of the things you miss most when living abroad is family and friends and it's always a real treat to have a visit from them (and not just because they bring you baked beans, teabags and Branston Pickle). I remember my parents' first visit – it was after several months with little contact outside our bubble. It was freezing cold, which we hadn't expected and were ill prepared for. However, we took advantage of the weather and drove up into the mountains where the snow had freshly fallen. It was magical and like driving through a scene from a Christmas card. We drove right to the top into the ski resort of Superbagnères. It was rather a treacherous drive up twisting mountain roads with sheer drops and hairpin bends. Mum had to close her eyes most of the journey, as she's not very good with heights. I was surprised at how deep the snow was for the time of year, with snow piled at the side of the road about 4' deep. It was worth the drive - the views from the top were fantastic. The clear blue sky contrasting against the crispness of the white snow looked unreal and the air was so clean you could almost taste it. My parents had started to fall in love with the area (who wouldn't) and several visits later, they decided to sell their flat in the UK and buy a home near us. I was over the moon as although we had managed without them for several years, we had all missed them and having them nearby would be so great.

They had no problems selling their flat of course, because the new owners of our guest house were more than happy to buy it. So, with that part of the transaction sorted, they were free to look for properties close to us. On their very first buying visit, they found and made an offer on a four-bed detached villa (for the same price as their one bed flat in Kent) about fifteen minutes from us. It was a villa style building, about thirty years old, built on a small plot of land with fantastic uninterrupted views over beautiful countryside with a backdrop of the Pyrenees. It was a bit cheaper than usual because it had a sitting tenant, but his tenancy only had one year left to run. They were advised that there should be no problem taking possession in a year and they of course had the benefit of the rent in that time while they waited. Tenancy agreements are usually renewed every three years and are heavily biased towards the tenant. It's said to be difficult to end a tenancy agreement, even if the tenant has stopped paying the rent. For instance, you can't evict a tenant during the winter months whether they've paid or not. There wasn't a problem with the tenant, but the owner of the house would have preferred to have it vacant as it would be easier to sell. However, she couldn't terminate the tenancy agreement until the end of the three years and only if she wanted to sell or gain access to the property as her primary residence. However, when my parents brought the property, they had no other home and it was to be their only residence. Therefore, they had the right to take possession of the property at the end of the three-year tenancy agreement which was to come to an end in one year from the date of completion. They decided to spend that year travelling with their caravan – they spent six months in Spain and six months in France. Whist in France they lived in their caravan in a park in the next town to us. It was lovely to have them nearby again. Luc was about eighteen months at the time and would spend a lot of time with them. He used to call them Granny and Granny, much to my dad's dismay. He kept saying "say, Grandad" to him and each time Luc would respond with "Granny", laugh mischievously and run away.

They enjoyed their year touring, but by the end of it they were eager and ready to settle into their new home.

It's common in France to use a *huissier* (bailiff) to collect rent and serve official notices to tenants. My parents carried on using the *huissier* that the previous owner had used to collect the rent and never had any problems. The tenant knew from the start that he had a year to find alternative accommodation and all the right notices were sent at the right time. A notice to quit the premises had to be served six months before the end of the tenancy agreement and all this was dealt with by the *huissier*. I've known lots of people have problems with French tenants, so the small percentage extra you pay for the services of a *huissier* is well worth it. The tenant dutifully left on the required date and they finally moved into their new French home in September 2007 and what a godsend for me that they did...

A 40ᵗʰ birthday surprise

On New Year's Eve 2006 and while my parents were between homes, I turned forty. By now, we were starting to build up a circle of friends and so we decided to celebrate it. Our previous two New Year's Eve nights in France had been a bit of a let-down. We had young children so couldn't really go out and there didn't seem to be anything going on locally anyway. As we'd stood at the door to see in the New Year, we'd been greeted with pitch black and complete silence. If the French celebrate New Year, they certainly were celebrating it a long way from us. We decided if we wanted to have fun on New Year's Eve, we had to create it ourselves, and my Fortieth Birthday seemed a fitting year to start. We organised the first of what was to become a yearly New Year's Eve event for all our friends and neighbours. We had about fifty guests come to share a buffet dinner, followed by dancing, fireworks and champagne. It was a great night and one I'll always remember. For my present, Gary gave me a card promising me a trip to Australia. Wow, how exciting, however I've yet to have the opportunity to take him up on this offer... a month or so after my fortieth Birthday I discovered I was pregnant again with our fifth child!

I really don't know how it happened – I suppose you'd have thought we'd have worked it out by now! It's not that we were trying for a girl, although many people think that after four boys, perhaps we were. I can't say I wasn't hoping for a girl although Gary was unsure what to do with a girl (his words not mine).

Anyway, once I got over the initial shock, I made an appointment to see my gynaecologist in Toulouse. He was very welcoming and friendly – I explained I was pregnant again; he made a joke about maybe it being a girl this time (at least that's what I thought he said). We went into his examining room, he gave me an internal (which I was quite used to by now), but then he gave me a smear test (the test given to women to check for cervical cancer). Now, this threw me a little, as I didn't think it was wise to be messing around unnecessarily at this early stage in the pregnancy. By the time I realised what he was doing, it was too late. I got dressed and went back to his office and he recommended I go for a mammogram and said it was best to go after my next period (not really sure why). "But I'm pregnant – do you mean wait until my periods return after the birth?" I said (in my best French of course). I had definitely told him I was pregnant when I first arrived, but perhaps he had misunderstood my accent. He looked a little confused, so he ushered me quickly back into the examining room and put a mini ultrasound scanner on my tummy and sure enough a tiny baby showed up on the computer screen. He then proceeded to write out prescriptions for ultrasound scans, blood tests, etc., and off I went. Less than a week later, I was horrified to find I had started losing some blood – whether this was caused by the smear test I will never know. I rang the gynaecologist and he recommended I go straight away for an ultrasound scan. The radiologist discovered a clot of blood in my uterus and strongly advised that I have complete bed rest for the next four weeks until I reached the 12 week stage and had my next ultrasound scan – if not I was likely to lose the baby. Four weeks in bed! How on earth was that going to be possible with lively two and five-year-old boys? However, Gary absolutely insisted that if that's what the doctor ordered, that was what was going to happen. He set me up in one of the *gîtes* and I stayed in bed for a month. It was incredibly boring – I read every book I could and tried watching French TV (as we didn't have Sky in the *gîte*) but discovered that there is nothing worth watching. We didn't have a laptop at the time, and I was lost without my computer. It was so difficult just lying there and hearing the bedlam exploding in the sitting room. Gary was brilliant and coped so well – he's so calm in a crisis and just does what has to be done. Our sacrifices paid off because when I went for my 12-week scan the blood clot had disappeared and I was given the all clear. She also asked me did I want to know what sex the baby was "*Non, merci*" was my reply – I wanted to imagine that it might be a little girl this time, for just a little longer.

Blood tests are carried out every month throughout the pregnancy here in France – unlike the UK where you normally only have one or two blood tests during the entire pregnancy (unless you have complications). In France, they have special *laboratoires analyse de sang*- you get your prescription for a blood test from the doctor or specialist, then you turn up at the lab as early as possible, without an appointment and on a day that suits you. It's usual to go early in the morning '*à jeun*' - which means you haven't had anything to drink or eat. After the blood has been taken, you are offered a coffee or hot chocolate and a croissant - very civilised. During the 4th month of pregnancy, there is a special blood test to calculate the risk of there being a problem with the baby. Unfortunately, after the routine blood test, I got a letter to say that I was "high risk" of there being a serious problem. They calculate the risk percentage based on a combination of the blood test results, the nuchal fold measurement (this is a measurement at the back of the neck which if taken at the right time during the pregnancy, can be a strong indicator of potential problems) and the patient's age (obviously the older you are the greater the risk of problems, although that doesn't necessary mean that there will be problems). It was all very worrying, and I had to go and see a genetic specialist in Toulouse. I understood that it was only an indicator and to be surer they would likely recommend me having an amniocentesis (an examination where they take a sample of amniotic fluid by putting a needle through the abdomen and into the uterus). I spent many sleepless nights tossing all the scenarios over in my mind - if I had an amnio, there was a slight risk of damaging the baby - was I prepared to take that risk when there could be nothing wrong? Also, if I found there was definitely something wrong, could I terminate the pregnancy at this stage after all the trouble we'd taken to save it? Was it fair to the other children if we had a disabled child? Could I cope with it? All these questions went round and round in my head. In the end, after a lot of soul searching, I decided that there was no way I could go ahead with a termination at this stage - whatever was wrong with the baby we would face it together as a family and so whatever the genealogist said, there was no point in having an amnio. I was much happier when I had come to this decision and so I went off to my appointment with my mind already made up. The genealogist asked lots of questions about family history and looked at all my test results. He advised having an amnio to make sure, but I told him I had decided against this. He explained that the nuchal fold test was fine, and only one of the two blood counters they use to assess the risk was lower than average – he said my age with the one abnormal test result was enough to put me statistically at risk, but there was a strong chance that there would be no problem with the baby. This was enough to put my mind at ease and I left there happy and didn't let it bother me anymore. What would be, would be.

At 32 weeks I had another routine scan and all seemed fine – the radiologist asked once again would I like to know what sex the baby was? This time I relented – it definitely felt different (I can't explain how) but if it really was a girl I wanted to go out and buy girly things in readiness for the birth. You can imagine after 18 years of boys' clothes and having a house cluttered with cars and swords, I wanted to make the most of buying pretty girly things! I know that sounds outrageously sexist, but I had spent 17 years as the only female in the house and it doesn't matter how much you try to be gender neutral, an awful lot of cars, swords and traditionally boy 'things' are strewn around the house. So, I took a deep breath and said, "*Oui, merci*" and mentally prepared myself for her to give me the news I was so used to hearing - it was another "*garçon*". I was stunned when she told me it was "*une fille*" – my heart started beating fast and the blood rushed to my cheeks. I was so filled with emotion that I could hold back no longer, and the tears streamed down my face. She looked really worried and asked if I was OK, I explained that it was just that I was so happy to be having a girl at last after four boys. Her concerned look was replaced by a large smile and I could detect a few tears welling up in her eyes too. It must be so rewarding to give people such good news; I would imagine that it's not always like that in her job. Now don't get me wrong, I love each and every one of my boys. They are all gorgeous and I am very proud of them, but I do feel a bit outnumbered at times. It's not easy being the only woman in a house full of testosterone, so it was nice to be evening out the statistics, if only slightly. I was over the moon - it was the best 40th birthday present Gary could ever have given me. I was supposed to be going on a trip to Australia, but after finding out I was pregnant and all the difficulties I had in the early stages, that had to be shelved permanently, but this was better than anything money could buy!

The rest of the pregnancy went smoothly and when I got the first contraction at 3.30pm one Sunday afternoon I called my parents (who were now living 10 minutes away) to come and watch the other children. We sped off to the hospital and I thought I was going to have her in the car on the way the contractions were so strong. When I arrived, I just had time to get an epidural done and within ½ an hour she was on her way - my gynaecologist had been called, but he didn't have time to get there and she had arrived by 6pm. Our beautiful baby girl at last - we named her Francesca (which means "from France") and she was absolutely perfect. She was born on 30th September 2007 - exactly three years (to the day) after we left England for our new life in France.

After pains

The hospitals here are generally very good, especially in the cities. You have a choice of either a general hospital or a *clinique*. A *clinique* is a private hospital, but everyone is entitled to choose to go to one and there are many to choose from in the cities. It seemed slightly alien at first, in the UK you only go to a private hospital if you have private medical insurance like BUPA or pay a lot of money. Here, everyone has the choice of a general hospital or one of the many *cliniques*. The only difference I can see is that the *cliniques* are often smaller and the consultants are usually a bit more expensive. For instance, to see a gynaecologist in the general hospital the standard rate is say 30 euros. However, a senior gynaecologist in a *clinique* might cost 40 euros. If you have a good top up insurance it should cover you for the extra, but if not, you have to pay the difference yourself. Other than that though, the charges for treatment and the stay in hospital are all covered as normal and don't usually cost much if anything extra.

I've unfortunately had many personal experiences with general hospitals and *cliniques* over the years which is I suppose par for the course when you have so many children. My first major personal experience (other than giving birth) happened a few months after Francesca was born. I didn't feel great after the birth, I felt weak, tired and as if I was in a bit of a haze, I couldn't think straight, and I put it down to lack of sleep and being an older mother. I was having some pelvic pain, but thought it was after pains, which seem to get worse with every child. I was also still losing blood eight weeks after the birth – which should have raised alarm bells perhaps to the gynaecologist on my seven-week check, had he asked. I should have mentioned it to him, but as I said, I wasn't really feeling myself. I soldiered on, feeling dreadful, until one day I felt so ill I couldn't get out of bed. A friend of mine popped in to see me.

"Nikki, you need to get yourself down t'doctors, sharpish!" She came from Manchester and they talk like that 'up North'.

She drove me to the local doctor's surgery but my usual doctor wasn't there, so I saw the replacement. After examining me, he wasn't happy with the pain I was having in my pelvis and prescribed a course of antibiotics, a pelvic scan and blood tests. He wrote out the prescriptions and made me appointments for that afternoon. The system in France is different to the UK. If a doctor considers you need x-rays or blood tests, he gives you a prescription and you then choose the radiology clinic or blood laboratory you wish to visit, which are often separate to the hospitals. You only normally need to wait a day or so to get an appointment, but in this case, because the doctor wanted the tests straight away, he made the appointments for me for that afternoon.

The doctor had made an appointment for me to see the radiologist in our local town. I'd always gone to Toulouse for scans during pregnancy but wasn't well enough to make the drive there, so I just did as I was told and went to the local radiologist. The radiologist wasn't really clear on what they could see but didn't seem to think it was anything urgent.

After the scan, I went to the laboratory for blood tests on the other side of town. I was very familiar with the setup here as I was used to monthly visits for blood tests during pregnancy. After a visit to the laboratory, you usually receive a copy of your tests through the post within a couple of days and now by email by the end of the day. However, I got a call early evening from the doctor – they had faxed the results through to him. The blood test showed I had a severe infection which would require intravenous antibiotics and a trip to hospital. He contacted the *clinique* in Toulouse where I had had the baby and spoke to my gynaecologist. He announced that there would be a space for me the following morning. In the meantime, I was advised to double the dose of the antibiotics I had been given, which I did.

That night was one the worst nights of my life. I'm not sure if it was the infection (I had a raging temperature and was in a lot of pain), or the double dose of antibiotics. Whatever it was I was tripping, and I didn't like where I was going! Whenever I closed my eyes the room would spin and spiral. I felt sure if I went to sleep, I would not wake up. I spent the night having strange hallucinations and crying about the fact I wouldn't be there for my children as they grew, got married and had children of their own.

Anyway, I made it through the night (obviously), and some friends took me to the hospital in Toulouse and dropped me off at the accident and emergency as instructed. I was immediately rigged up to a drip and then told to wait in the waiting room until a bed was ready. Four hours later, I was still sitting in the waiting room with a drip attached to my arm, feeling like death, not only from being ill, but also lack of sleep. I could hear the receptionist making lots of phone calls and I was starting to realise they must be about me. It transpired that they didn't have a bed for me after all and after phoning several different private clinics, the only hospital that could take me was the general hospital in Toulouse. An ambulance arrived to take me off and insisted on carrying me on a stretcher. I felt a bit of a fake. "I can walk", I said, but no, they had to take me on the trolley. I felt dreadfully hot and dizzy and was still spaced out, drugged up, in pain and alone.

We arrived at the hospital and the ambulance driver turned to me and said (in French) "That's 45 euros please" I couldn't quite believe it. There I was, at death's door (or so it felt) and he was asking me to pay. I had no money on me, but I had my *carte vitale* – wouldn't that count? No, I had to pay then and there. I fumbled for my cheque book, not quite believing what was happening to me and shakily wrote out the cheque. Did I really just wait all that time on an uncomfortable chair, get trundled off to another hospital and then get asked to pay for the privilege? Was it some sort of weird drug induced trip or did that really just happen? No, it seemed it really did!

Once I got into the hospital, I then had to tell the whole story of what had happened, symptoms, etc., again to another medical team. They immediately carried out another scan and explained that it was apparent I had some sort of swelling internally in my pelvic area and the only way they could really see what was going on would be to operate. They decided to carry out the operation the following morning as it was early evening by now (I had been dropped off at the *clinique* at 11am). Around 7pm I had finally been given a private room with bathroom and a comfortable bed. It was such a relief; all I wanted to do was sleep.

I was taken early next morning to the operating theatre. It was a bit scary as I'd never had an operation before. I'd only ever been in hospital to give birth. They wheeled me down, put a needle in my arm and before I knew what was going on it was all over and I was in the recovery room. They explained to me I had an abscess on my fallopian tube the size of an orange and they had removed my right fallopian tube and ovary. "Don't worry though, the other one's fine and you can still have another child". I smiled weakly at them while in my head I was thinking "Couldn't you have taken the other as well!" Having more children had never been further from my mind.

I was in hospital for about five days. The staff were very efficient and friendly, the hospital was clean, the room was comfortable and peaceful and so I really couldn't fault the care I received there. However, the atmosphere of the private *clinique* I stayed in with my pregnancies was even better. Just the sheer size of the general hospital is slightly off-putting, whereas the *cliniques* are smaller. The consultants in the general hospital are more pressed for time and you have to wait longer for appointments. The general hospitals also have a lot of trainee doctors whereas the *cliniques* don't, which is also one of the reasons you pay more in a *clinique*. There was at least a two-month waiting list when I tried to make an appointment with the consultant gynaecologist, but the consultant at the private clinic took about a month (unless it was an emergency of course). At the private *clinique* they seem to have more time for you and treat you almost like an old friend. I suppose they have to justify you paying more somehow. I'm splitting hairs here really. I was spoilt in the private *cliniques* I used for my pregnancy. General hospital care in Toulouse was great and far superior to my experiences of hospitals in the UK. The last time I was in hospital in England was after the birth of James. The hospital was dirty, the wards overcrowded and understaffed. I had ants crawling all over my grapes and had to wander around the ward trying to find water as it had not been filled all day and there was no one about to ask.

When opportunity knocks!

Nine months later, we decided to take our first holiday in the four years since moving to France. The first couple of years, we had so much to do and it sort of felt like a permanent holiday in a way, but although we lived in beautiful surroundings, we could never fully relax at home – there was always so much to do! We decided to hire a campervan and tour along the southeast coast of France and into Italy. It wasn't as if we had loads of money. The business was doing OK, although we were still living hand to mouth, but the *MSA (Mutualité Sociale Agricole* or social security for agricultural and horticultural workers) were offering 30 euros per child per day towards a family holiday for those in a low-income bracket. Having four children qualifying for this offer gave us the opportunity to hire the campervan and take a family holiday for the first time in years. The last proper holiday we had had was when James was a baby – he was now (at that time) six. We were all really looking forward to the holiday and planning the route and places to visit. It had been a particularly wet and miserable June across Europe, and we were longing for some sunshine. I kept checking the short- and long-term weather forecasts and it was heavy rain across France and Italy. I spoke to a colleague in Monaco and she confirmed the weather there was unseasonably bad. Hmmm, touring for two weeks in a campervan with four kids in the rain – a recipe for disaster, I think! We started searching, not for places of interest so much as searching for the sun and it seemed the only place within a reasonable travelling distance was Spain. Up until this point we hadn't really thought much of Spain. We'd had a cheap holiday in Majorca pre-children which gave us the impression of a beautiful island spoilt by tourism (largely British) and not particularly welcoming locals. We had ruled out Spain in our minds as not for us. But, needs must, and we needed a holiday and the sun, so Spain it was.

We planned our route across the Pyrenees and into Spain and headed off aiming for Valencia. As we crossed the border into Spain, the weather just started getting better and better, only two hours away from home and we had stopped at the roadside to have lunch and bask in the warmth of the sun. We took our time travelling down across Spain, the journey was fantastic, the twisting turns through the Pyrenean mountains revealing breath-taking views with every turn, beautiful lakes, abandoned villages made way to the open plains of orange groves and olive trees. Although Spain is only an hour's drive from our home to the border, you really know you're in a different country. It just got hotter and hotter to our great relief.

The campervan suited us very well – the youngest were six, three and nine months old, so it was handy to stop for toilet breaks and food without having to find somewhere suitable. Cups of tea whenever we fancied and everything to hand. We took our time travelling down across Spain and we hit the Tarragona coast in the Costa Daurada about 10pm. By this time, it was dark, and we were all tired and needed to sleep. We stopped at the first campsite we came across, found a pitch right at the bottom of the site and bedded down for the night. Gary and I slept in the double above the cab with baby Frankie between us and James, Luc and Ryan slept in the double at the back. That way the beds were always made up and we didn't have to mess about with rearranging the dining area to sleep.

When we awoke in the morning, we couldn't believe our luck. We were parked right on the edge of the most beautiful sandy beach – no shops, no high-rise hotels, just beautiful sand, sea and a little beach bar – perfect! Although not luxurious, the campsite had a pool, children's play area, restaurant and shop for your essentials. Gary decided to go on the scooter we'd brought with us and explore the area a little – it was much easier than packing up the van and driving around. He was gone a couple of hours. The boys played in the sand, I set up Frankie's travel cot outside the van under the awning and she happily sat and played in there while I sat with a coffee and soaked up the warmth of the sun. Ahhh, this was the life. How lucky were we to find this perfect spot?

Gary came back really excited. "You'll never guess what I've found Nicks".

"Did you find a garden centre by any chance?" I inquired.

"How did you guess?". It wasn't difficult. Whenever we went anywhere, Gary would always hunt out a local garden centre/nursery and have a look at what they sell. It was his passion.

"It's unbelievable, you'll have to come and see. The quality of the plants, it's amazing and the prices...."

He was buzzing. We went back several times over the course of the holiday taking note of the stock, prices and how much to deliver to France, minimum orders, etc. He wasn't sure what he was going to do about it but felt sure there was an opportunity there somewhere. We are both great believers in fate. It had been fate that brought us to this place, we hadn't even been thinking of coming to Spain. The seed was sown and over the following months we discussed lots of ways we might capitalise on what Gary had discovered. Our biggest problem was money or lack of it. We had no spare cash, no savings at all. We were living hand to mouth; it was so frustrating.

There was an empty business premises in our local town – it had been empty for about a year. "You know, I think that would make an excellent site for a garden centre", Gary posed to me one day.

"Yes, I suppose so, but how could we do that without money?"

"I've got a feeling about this, let's just give them a call and ask how much the rent would be – there's no harm in asking". That was true enough, so we asked Ryan to call the owner and arrange a meeting with him at the premises. He gave us a price for renting 1/3 of the building and all the land. It was tempting, but we still had a long way to go.

Business rentals here in France work on a 3,6,9-year basis. Once you commit yourself to a rental you have the right to rent it for up to nine years on the lease. You are committed to at least three years. At the end of those three years you can give up the lease without penalty (provided you give the landlord six months' notice in writing) and then you are committed to another three years and then another. The tenant has a get-out clause every three years, the landlord must let you rent it for the full nine years if you choose to do so. So, we knew we were committing ourselves for at least three years if we decided to go ahead. It was a big decision and a big commitment.

"How on earth are we going to fund this Gary, we have no money." I reasoned.

"Let's just talk to the bank, they might let us borrow it". It was worth a try I suppose. We had run our landscaping business for three years and the turnover had doubled each year. We also had our house with no mortgage. The bank manager didn't say no, he seemed quite positive and asked for a copy of our business plan. Our accountant helped us to formulate it. There was such a lot to consider, starting a garden centre completely from scratch. It was hard, but exciting at the same time.

The bank manager said yes in principal, it just had to be processed, which should take about four to six weeks. It was early February and Gary knew from his experience of running a garden centre in the UK that April/May was the busiest time. We really needed to be opened by April or it wasn't worth starting until the Autumn.

"Is this feasible?" we asked the manager. He gave a Celtic shrug and said he couldn't see why not.

So, the whirlwind started. We knew we had to act fast and if the money wasn't going to be available until the beginning of April, we had to have everything organised and in place for then. We hunted for suppliers, put in orders, scraped together the deposit for the premises. It was in a bit of a state, but the landlord let us in a month earlier to clean up and paint everything. We decided on a name, got a website, designed a logo with the help of an artist friend. We had signs made, prepared the land ready for the plants and bought some second-hand desks for the office and to make a counter. There was so much to think about and plan.

At the end of March, we had a call from the bank to come and sign some papers. We were so pleased and took this as a sign we were nearly there. We were seen by another guy at the bank who explained he was in charge of the insurance. He didn't have a clue what our loan was even for. He pulled out the file and started asking us the most basic questions.

"We've already gone through all this. Aren't we here to sign for the loan?"

"Oh no, this is the first stage of the process- filling in the insurance forms and application, it then goes off to head office for approval.

"But we thought all this had been done and we were just waiting approval – how long will it be now?"

"Oh at least four to six weeks" came the reply. My heart sank, Gary's turned to fire – he was absolutely livid. The poor chap must have wondered what had hit him.

"This is absolutely ridiculous; how does anyone ever get on in business in this country. We were told four to six weeks, six weeks ago. I'm trying to start a business here. We have to be open in a few weeks or there's no point. What's the matter with you people!" I had to try and translate this to the bewildered guy. I don't think they normally get this reaction. Most French people know that four to six weeks actually means at least three months. What particularly incensed Gary was that the file had been sitting on the bank manager's desk for six weeks and nothing had been done with it.

It was a massive blow, even if we changed banks, it would still take at least another four to six weeks. We explained the situation to our accountant, who advised us to go to another bank. This manager was more switched on and she was confident if anyone could do something for us, he could. We booked an appointment to see him and explained our business plan and how we'd been let down by our previous bank. He perused the business plan and asked some pertinent and relevant questions (which is more than our other bank manager had). He seemed keen to help us out. He was impressed by our enthusiasm and track record. We had plenty of landscaping work coming up, so it wasn't as though the business was being started from nothing. We had lots of potential customers already from previous and current clients and gardening club members. He said yes in principle and the loan would take four to six weeks to arrive. He felt confident he could get it through in four weeks. Encouraged, we ploughed on with our plans and preparations, bought stock on 30 or 60-days credit where we could. We set our opening day as 9th May – a bit later than we'd hoped, but still enough time to capitalise on the busy season we felt.

The opening day was less than a week away and we still hadn't got our money through. I spoke to M. Lasserre the bank manager on the phone.

"Is it going through OK, we need to open?"

"I'm still waiting on something, but it really shouldn't be long now". We had to make a decision. Our main stock was coming from the supplier in Spain – Olive trees, Palms and Mediterranean shrubs. It was essential to our success. It was what made us different. This shipment had to be ordered and paid for now if were to have any chance of delivery before the opening day in one week. We couldn't afford to wait a moment longer and so we decided to bite the bullet and booked an appointment to choose the stock in Spain and booked the transport for the Wednesday. It was a risk and edge of your seat stuff. I couldn't quite believe I was booking a lorry for 6000 euros worth of plants when we hadn't yet got the finance in place for at the time. It was very out of character for me, but we had to take a chance if we were going to have any hope of opening the following Saturday.

We left on the Tuesday for Spain and called into the bank on the way to see if the Manager could do anything for us. His eyes nearly popped out of his head when we explained we were on our way to Spain to buy the stock and we hadn't the money yet. We explained we had no choice; it was now or never. Was there anything he could do, an overdraft or something to tide us over until the loan came through. You could tell he admired our guts and really wanted to help us out. He offered to arrange a short-term stock loan to cover the cost of the Spanish stock and the other essentials we needed to get us up and running while we were waiting for the main loan to arrive. He was our saviour. We couldn't quite believe it. So off we went to Spain with a huge sigh of relief knowing that we would have the money in the bank the next day to pay for all we ordered.

It was a whirlwind 12-hour round trip and half a day there choosing the stock. Looking back, I'm not sure how we managed it now. Once back there was no rest – we had to get the premises looking like a Garden Centre and ready for the opening. We knew it would be tight – the shipment arrived just a day before opening. We called on all our friends from the gardening club to lend a hand and true to form they came along and helped us label, shift, move, arrange, display. By some miracle we managed to get everything ready for the opening. I'm not sure how, we were having hardly any sleep – there just weren't enough hours in the day. It's amazing where you find the strength when you need it.

Our opening day went well, particularly as we only knew about four days before that it was going to go ahead. We decided to have an official opening day a couple of weeks later, where we invited our clients, gardening club members, friends and neighbours to a free buffet, drink and had speeches thanking various people for all their help in making the opening possible. This went really well and is probably one of our proudest moments. We had achieved the seemingly impossible, against all the odds our new business Kingdom Vegetal was born.

I'd like to say, "and we all lived happily ever after", but of course life is never that simple. The first year of the business was great, but it cost an enormous amount of money and the first five years or so were very tough both with the business and our personal lives, but that's another story...

Postscript

I was loading the shopping onto the conveyor belt at the supermarket checkout. The same supermarket I had entered on that very first day we had moved to France when I'd nearly been locked in over lunch, all those years ago. Only now it was much bigger and smarter after renovation works a few years back and it even stayed open at lunchtime – there's progress for you! I was lost in my own thoughts of what we were going to have for dinner or something when I heard someone call my name.

"Nikki, how are you doing?" I looked up to see a scruffy guy with long dreadlocks, baggy trousers and open toe sandals smiling at me. I narrowed my eyes, desperately searching my memory to recall who this guy was.

"It's me, Frans!" he'd obviously noticed I was struggling to recognise him, and he came and kissed me on both cheeks.

"Hello, I'm sorry Frans, I was miles away" I flustered, but what I was really thinking was, oh my god what's happened to that clean-cut estate agent who sold us our house all those years ago? "How are you, we haven't seen you for ages", I added.

"I'm okay, gave up my estate agency job a few years back and I'm just doing a bit of this and that now. How are you doing? It's so good to see you. How's Gary? How are the kids?"

"They're all really good thanks. Did you know we have another now – a little girl this time."

"No, really? So that's five. Wow. And I hear you've opened a Garden Centre. How's it going?"

"It's good thanks, lots of work, but we're enjoying it."

"You know when I saw you two in the beginning in that great big mill, with all that work, the kids and the baby, I said to myself, they won't last here more than a year." He shook his head incredulously

"Really?" that surprised me, if that was how he'd felt he'd never let on.

181

"You know, you've done so well to make it here, not so many people do. You should be proud. I'm really pleased for you." He looked at me with such genuine warmth I knew this was coming from the heart. I smiled, not really knowing how to respond to this revelation.

"Well, I'd best be going. Good luck with the business." He took my hand with both of his and shook it warmly.

"Thanks, and you" I smiled.

He went to leave and then just as he passed through the automatic doors he turned back, raised his arm in parting and called out "Greetings to Gary!" as the door slid shut and he was gone...

Glossary of French Terms

Aire	A service area provided on main roads
A jeun	Without eating or drinking (when going for blood tests)
Allocations familiales	Family allowance
Anglais(e)	English
Attestation de vente	Proof of purchase of a house
Auberge	An inn, and is also sometimes used to refer to a restaurant
Baguette	Long, thin bread stick
Bastide	A fortified village or town
CAF (Caisse d'Allocations Familiales)	The government office that handles services and benefits for families and individuals. Many of these benefits are revenue tested, some are not.
Caillou	Stone
Carte de séjour	Residency permit
Carte grise	Registration document
Carte verte	Car insurance certificate
Carte Vitale	Health insurance card
Cassis	Blackcurrant

Cèpes	A very popular and usually expensive type of wild mushroom
Ceinture	Seatbelt
Certificat d'inscription	Permission to start school given by the local mayor
Certificat de radiation	A certificate to confirm your child is no longer inscribed to the school
Certificat de scolarité	A certificate certifying that your child is enrolled in school
Chambre d'hôtes	Bed and breakfast
Chanterelles	Variety of wild mushroom
Clinique	Private, specialised hospital or medical centre
Colombage	Half timbered
Compromis de vente	Preliminary contract signed when buying a house in France
Confit de canard	Duck legs preserved with salt, herbs and spices
Contrôle technique (CT)	MOT
Cotisations sociales	The French equivalent of UK National Insurance contributions
Covoiturage	Car sharing

CPAM (Caisse Primaire d'Assurance Maladie)	Social Security
Crème de Cassis	Blackcurrant liqueur
Croissant	Crescent shaped pastry
Débroussailleuse	Brush cutter
Délesteur	A computerised electrical box
Dépot vente or Troc	Second-hand shops where you can take your furniture or other items to be sold and they sell them for you and take a commission when sold
Directrice/Directeur d'Ecole	Head Teacher
Echographie	Ultrasound
EDF (Electricité de France)	The main electric supplier in France
Farine à gâteaux	Sifted flour for making cakes (no raising agent)
Fauchage	Team of council workers who are responsible for cutting the hedgerows
(Une) fille	Girl
Floc de Gascogne	A fortified wine

Flute	A long stick of bread, thicker than a *baguette*
Foie gras	A specialty food product made of the liver of force-fed ducks or geese
Fonctionnaire	Civil servant
(Un) garçon	Boy
Gîte	A property used for short-term rental
Gîtes de France	A network, a brand and a label of accommodation in France and in Europe
Hotel de Ville	Town Hall
Huissier	Bailiff
Kinésithérapeute	Physiotherapist
Laboratoires d'analyse de sang	Blood test laboratories
Maigret de canard	Duck breasts
Maire	Mayor
Mairie	Mayor's office, or Town hall
Malade/Maladie	Ill/Illness
Maternelle	Preschool/kindergarden
• *Petite section*	Youngest section in preschool for children aged two and a half to three

- *Moyenne section*   The middle class in preschool for children aged four to five
- *Grande section*   The top class in preschool for children aged five to six

Médicaments   Medicines

Menu du jour   A reasonably priced three-course midday meal usually comprising an entrée followed by the *plat du jour*, a dessert and often a ¼ litre of wine included in the price

Menu gourmand   Gourmet menu

Météo-France   French weather site

Monophase   Single phase electric system

Moulin   Mill or watermill

MSA (Mutualité Sociale Agricole)   Social Security organisation for agricultural and horticultural workers

Mutuelle   Top-up medical insurance

Notaire   Solicitor

(Un) oeuf   Egg

Ordonnance   Prescription

Pain au chocolat (or Chocolatine)   Round pastry filled with chocolate

Pain au raisin   Pastry filled with raisins

Péage   Toll road

Pendre la crémaillère or *pendaison de crémaillère*	Housewarming
Péridurale	Epidural
Permis de conduire	Driving licence
Pied de mouton	Variety of wild mushroom
Pigeonnièr	Pigeon house
Plat du jour	the main dish (or dishes) of the day
Pompiers	Fire brigade
Potager	Vegetable garden
Préfecture	The main governmental administrative office for things like visas, car registrations and driving licences.
Prime à la naissance	A one-off payment given during the seventh month of pregnancy to help buy essentials
Prise de sang	Blood tests
Royaume-Uni	United Kingdom
SAFER (Société d'Aménagement Foncier et d'Etablissement Rural)	A government agency that has the right of first purchase on many rural properties that come onto the market in France.
Sous-préfecture	A sub office to the main (See *Préfecture)*
Terre de bruyère	Ericaceous (acid) compost

A family moving to France

Tondeuse	Lawn mower
Triphase	Three-phrase electric system
Troc or dépot vente	Second-hand shops where you can take your furniture or other items to be sold and they sell it for you and take a commission when it is sold
Trompettes de la mort	Variety of wild mushroom
Tronçonneuse	Chainsaw
Vide-grenier	Literally "Empty hayloft" and is like a British « Boot fair », second-hand sale.

Message from the author

I hope you have enjoyed this book and have found it both useful and entertaining. I would really appreciate it if you could take the time to post a review on either Amazon or Good Reads as it will help others to discover how you found the book.

If you have any suggestions of topics you would find useful in coming books or blogposts, then please feel free to contact me. You can connect with me on Twitter, Instagram or Facebook @AmotherinFrance.

To receive regular updates, news and special offers please sign-up to my newsletter on www.amotherinfrance.com

I look forward to connecting with you in the future.

All my best,

Nikki McArthur

Printed in Great Britain
by Amazon

31250151R00116